MICHIGAN
AND THE
CIVIL WAR

MICHIGAN
AND THE
CIVIL WAR

A Great and Bloody Sacrifice

JACK DEMPSEY

THE
History
PRESS

Published by The History Press
Charleston, SC 29403
www.historypress.net

All photos are courtesy of the Archives of Michigan.

First published 2011
Second printing 2011
Third printing 2011
Fourth printing 2012

Manufactured in the United States

ISBN 978.1.60949.173.4

Library of Congress Cataloging-in-Publication Data

Dempsey, Jack, 1952-
Michigan and the Civil War : a great and bloody sacrifice / Jack Dempsey.
p. cm.
Includes bibliographical references and index.
ISBN 978-1-60949-173-4
1. Michigan--History--Civil War, 1861-1865. 2. United States--History--Civil War, 1861-
1865. I. Title.
E514.D46 2011
977.4'03--dc22
2010050612

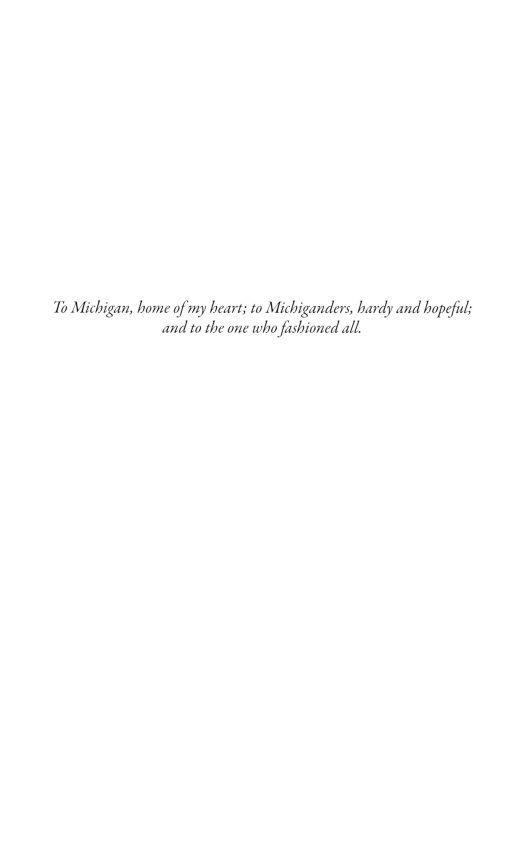

To Michigan, home of my heart; to Michiganders, hardy and hopeful; and to the one who fashioned all.

CONTENTS

CONTENTS

Preface

A half-century ago, Civil War author and native Michigander Bruce Catton delivered the eleventh annual Lewis Cass lecture, when he received an honorary doctorate of humanities from Wayne State University in Detroit. His remarks were entitled *Michigan's Past and the Nation's Future*. As was typical with Catton, the speech was thoughtful and poetic. It concluded with this glimpse of the road ahead:

> *It is here we need the kind of courage which a study of our own past can give us. We need boldness and we need imagination—the boldness that finds materials for victory in the moment when the battle seems lost; the imagination that can look beyond the present crisis to the world that is waiting for us to enter it. We are not fighting a rear-guard action, after all. Our heritage contains the vision, the faith and the courage by which this dangerous path can be turned into an avenue toward the future. Man is still God's instrument on earth; his dreams are still things that can survive him and become real.*

Michigan continues its wandering journey on that path. Its past—including the last dispiriting decade—is prelude to a future that still depends for success, as it did in 1959, on imagination, boldness, faith and courage.

The Civil War generation of Michiganders—black, white and red, men, women and children—helped save the nation during its greatest crisis. Providing stalwart leadership, critical manpower, abundant materiel and political support for the Union cause, Michigan was a true blue state. Its people became extraordinary instruments of ultimate victory, yielding the promise of a new birth of freedom that today continues to be fulfilled. Even its own citizens have too often overlooked Michigan's inestimable contributions during the War era. Current and future generations can take confidence and inspiration from the role Michigan played during the ordeal; beyond its lakes and borders, others may find lessons from the Great Lake State helpful in their own crisis.

We can still be extraordinary instruments.

Chapter 1

ROCKETS' RED GLARE

The firing of Confederate cannons was unrelenting on this second day of the battle. From positions all around Charleston Harbor, forty-three hostile guns were trained on the United States fort on a man-made island, raining down solid shot and hot fire. The overmatched Federal garrison inside Fort Sumter fought back. Able to service less than ten guns, with the bulk of the force furiously stitching together ammunition bags to help the gunners keep firing back, the eighty-five members of the Federal contingent did their best for Old Glory as it whipped in the whirlwind above the ramparts. The sun was high this Saturday, April 13, 1861, but it was the heat and smoke from Rebel projectiles exploding on the parade ground that wore down the fort's defenders.

The last of the cooked rations had been served at daybreak to the officers and men of the garrison. Now they would have to subsist on dried provisions, assuming their ammunition and the structure held out. One Rebel gun fired every quarter-hour during the night, and the full Confederate firepower opened up soon after dawn on day two. This day's bombardment had better accuracy and greater effect. The walls and casemate took a fearful pounding; explosions of shot and shell shook the fort as in an earthquake. Mortar rounds sailed high into the air and plummeted almost vertically into the open space within the fort, endangering anyone who emerged from shelter. One shell arced through the roof of the officers' quarters, and within moments, the building was fully engaged in flames. Men rushed to protect the ammunition and magazine from explosion. A glance at a timepiece would show it was near one o'clock in the afternoon on this desperate day.

Suddenly, the main flagstaff toppled and gave way, succumbing to the damage from two Rebel shell hits. Broad stripes and bright stars fell to the parade ground, and one of the officers sprang into action. "Lieutenant Hall rescued the precious bunting before it took fire," it would be recounted; that would be Second Lieutenant Norman Hall, United States Army, formerly of Monroe, Michigan. With the assistance of two others, Hall raised the shot-strewn banner onto a temporary flagpole, where it spread out its folds in the breeze and began to fly defiantly over the fortress again. Hall's feat of bravery was but the latest act of service to his country during the tense times leading up to the battle. He had yet to reach his twenty-fifth birthday.

Norman Jonathan Hall had graduated from the United States Military Academy at West Point less than two years earlier. Ranking thirteenth in the 1859 class of twenty-two cadets, he would become twenty-two that year. Born

Norman Hall.

in New York State on March 4, 1837, Hall moved with his family to London Township, Michigan, a bit west of Monroe, when he was still a boy. On March 19, 1854, he received an appointment to West Point from Michigan approved by the secretary of war, Jefferson Davis, the future Confederate president. Upon graduation, Hall received an appointment as second lieutenant in the Fourth U.S. Artillery and became ranking second lieutenant in the First U.S. Artillery on January 10, 1860.

He was assigned to the Charleston, South Carolina garrison on September 1, 1860, where he served as post adjutant and in acting capacities as assistant quartermaster and commissary of subsistence. As November approached, it had proven more and more difficult to obtain supplies in Charleston because of tensions over the coming presidential outcome. Once Abraham Lincoln was elected, South Carolina passed an ordinance of secession—official withdrawal from the United States of America—portending a total interruption of supply, and worse. The commander of the garrison, Kentucky-born major Robert Anderson, took stock of the anti-Federal sentiments of the populace. On the day after Christmas, he relocated his small force from a position on shore to Fort Sumter in the middle of Charleston Harbor. Since this action failed to account for South Carolina's newly declared independent status, all of Charleston erupted. Within a short span, South Carolina's military forces occupied the Federal installations ringing the harbor around the island fortress. Anderson had bought some time, but he had also stirred up a hornets' nest.

On January 9, Anderson pressed Hall into more hazardous duty than a quartermaster was accustomed to facing. He was ordered to carry a dispatch to Governor Pickens seeking information on South Carolina's intentions. After delivering the message and receiving a response (which was uncooperative), Hall and his small party returned to the dock for the return trip to Sumter. They encountered a boisterous crowd who were agitated about a rumored Federal plan to attack the city. Hall tried to make assurances that no such plan existed, but the angry confrontation between Southerners and a uniformed Army officer was the latest signal that peace at Charleston was only temporary. Several days later, Hall and the South Carolina attorney general set out by train for Washington, D.C., as emissaries of their superiors to see if authorities in the capital might devise a resolution of the crisis. The trip did not succeed. The outgoing Buchanan government would not evacuate the fort, but neither would it reinforce its garrison. The status quo would persist.

After Lincoln's inauguration on March 4, 1861, the new government requested Anderson to report on his strength and provide recommendations for a course of action. On March 15, Lincoln and his cabinet, General Winfield Scott, commander of the U.S. Army, and other military officers gathered in the White House to hear the report. It revealed that subsistence would be exhausted within a few weeks and insisted that twenty thousand troops were needed to hold the fort. One of Anderson's aides, Abner Doubleday of later baseball fame, estimated ten thousand were necessary. Lieutenant Hall's plan was also laid before the meeting, and it was not nearly as pessimistic: only two or three thousand soldiers were needed, and they could be delivered by small ships under cover of the fort's guns. Whether Hall's input convinced the Lincoln administration not to evacuate the fort is uncertain. History does record, however, that within several days a decision was made: the fort would not be surrendered, and provisions would be forwarded to sustain its defenders.

On April 1, the guns at Fort Moultrie fired on a vessel bearing the U.S. flag as it attempted to enter Charleston Harbor. Major Anderson observed the incident and polled his officers on what response should be made. Lieutenant Hall and four others urged firing back, but Anderson sided with those who urged no hostile action at this delicate juncture. Within days the situation escalated further. Hall was unable to obtain further supplies, and the South Carolina and Confederate governments were moving toward imposing a deadline for surrender of Sumter. When informed of the resupply expedition that was on its way to Charleston, the governments reached their decision. On April 11, three Confederate officers rowed out to the fort to deliver a demand for evacuation. Again Anderson convened his staff, and this time all the officers concurred in refusing the ultimatum. Anderson replied accordingly—except that he left the door slightly ajar as to how diminishing supplies might soon force him to leave rather than starve. Shortly after midnight, four Confederate officers paid another trip and inquired more specifically about Anderson's intentions. Would he firmly commit to a date to abandon Fort Sumter? Yes, he replied, by April 15—if not by then reinforced, resupplied or instructed by Washington to undertake some other course of action. The Confederates caucused and responded, in accordance with their instructions, at around 3:30 a.m.: the time for negotiation had ended. The fort would be fired upon in one hour.

Rockets' Red Glare

At 4:30 a.m. on Friday, a signal gun went off. Cannonades immediately commenced from all Confederate positions. Anderson divided his officers into three reliefs of two hours each to service Fort Sumter's guns and returned fire. Outgunned, outnumbered and outprovisioned, the garrison's only hope was that the relief expedition would run the gauntlet into the harbor and attempt resupply. It did not. By midafternoon on Saturday, the American flag had fallen, albeit temporarily until Hall raised it again, and provisions were running out. Southern emissaries soon appeared to inquire if striking the banner meant a signal to surrender. Although the Stars and Stripes were flying again, Anderson decided that his force had defended it long enough and—if permitted to evacuate safely, saluting the flag and removing it as they left—said he would abandon Fort Sumter to the Confederacy. Agreement was reached; on Sunday, April 14, the Federal garrison saluted the colors one final time, left the fort and boarded a vessel for New York, where it arrived three days later.

The nation hailed the heroes of Fort Sumter, chiefly Anderson. An engraving of him with six of his officers appeared soon in a *Harper's Weekly* pictorial, circulating their images to the largest weekly periodical readership in America. What were the whereabouts of a seventh officer? Hall was already on assignment in Michigan to help raise and lead a regiment of infantry to reclaim Federal installations being appropriated by secessionists all across the South. Major Anderson, however, did not overlook his aide, for in an after-action report on promotions and commendations for service during the Charleston crisis, he called attention to the role of Lieutenant Hall "to whom I was greatly indebted."

Norman Jonathan Hall would reappear in other key roles on the Union side during the next several years of the escalating conflict that had begun in the South Carolina harbor. He would again be in harm's way now that a great civil war, long feared, had begun. Though miles away, Michigan—in the person of one of her brave sons—had been on the firing line already.[1]

Chapter 2

THE COMING FURY

On January 26, 1837, long-awaited good news came to the people of Michigan Territory.[2] President Andrew Jackson signed legislation admitting Michigan into the Union as the twenty-sixth state. Its entry marked a doubling in the number of the original thirteen states, but superstition was not a cause of the more than two-year delay in achieving statehood. A border dispute with the state of Ohio, resolved only when Michigan relinquished its claim to Toledo and its Lake Erie harbor while accepting the bulk of the Upper Peninsula, prompted the detention.

Under the leadership of territorial governor Stevens T. Mason, who believed Michigan qualified for admission, steps were taken in 1834 and 1835 to demonstrate that condition. A census revealed that Michigan had more than enough population; Mason called for and helped direct a convention to draft a constitution. The effort went so far as the design of a great seal of the state to be used for official documents. To this day, it bears the date of 1835,[3] representative of a populace who would beat down the door to enter into the Union.

Michigan came in as a free state. Ironically, it once had been slave territory because of French and British antecedents. Slavery existed in the Great Lakes territory at the formation of the nation; for example, the estate of William Macomb—namesake of Michigan's third largest county—included twenty-six slaves. Contemporary histories described how the French aided Native American allies by keeping as slaves the enemies of those tribes. Statehood did not, however, commence eradication of the practice. That came earlier.

In 1787, the same year the U.S. Constitution was written and proposed to the original thirteen states, the Continental Congress approved a measure determining the future of the territory north and west of the Ohio River. This "Northwest Ordinance" decreed that from three to five new states would be created and join the Union "on an equal footing with the original States in all respects whatever." A major difference, however, was found in this language: "[t]here shall be neither slavery nor involuntary servitude in the said territory, otherwise than in the punishment of crimes whereof the party shall have been duly convicted."[4] Although outlawed, it was not until the British surrendered control of the territory in 1796 that the declaration was other than a paper statement. The antislavery provision made it into the ordinance in an interesting way. According to its chief drafter, he "had no idea the States would agree to the sixth Art. prohibiting slavery, as only [Massachusetts] of the Eastern States was present—and therefore omitted it in the draft—but finding the House favorably disposed on the subject, after we had completed the other parts I moved the art.—which was agreed to without opposition."[5] A strange twist of history helped make Michigan a land of liberty for all.

From such a serendipitous origin, the theme found its way into the original Michigan Constitution of 1835 in the ordinance-based phrasing of Article IX: "Neither slavery nor involuntary servitude shall ever be introduced into this state, except for the punishment of crimes of which the party shall have been duly convicted."[6] A year after the constitution process was complete and just months before statehood, delegates from southeast Michigan gathered at the First Presbyterian Church in Ann Arbor on November 10, 1836, for what they called an "Anti-Slavery State Convention."[7] The outcomes included establishment of the Michigan State Anti-Slavery Society, a series of resolutions attacking the institution of slavery in the Southern and border states and a decision to begin publication of an antislavery newspaper.

It would take some time—and some courage—to go to press, given events in a neighboring jurisdiction. In the fall of 1837 in Illinois, a proslavery crowd murdered publisher Elijah Lovejoy over his abolitionist articles. Within the next several years, though, three different antislavery publications would emerge in Michigan. Brothers William and Nicholas Sullivan published the first, the *American Freeman*, in Jackson in 1838. The next year, Seymour Treadwell began publishing the *Michigan Freeman*. Theodore Foster and the Reverend Guy Beckley launched the *Signal of Liberty* in April 1841 with operations above a shop on Broadway Avenue in Ann Arbor. This weekly publication included minutes from antislavery meetings across the state. All three papers sought to convince the rest of Michigan to support the nationwide abolition of slavery.[8]

Not all in the state concurred. Having three electoral votes upon its admission, Michigan initially supported presidential candidates of the antiabolition Democratic Party. Martin Van Buren carried Michigan in 1836, James Polk in 1840, native son Lewis Cass in 1848 and Franklin Pierce in 1852. While more Michiganders were voting for platforms that promised noninterference with slavery, others were aiding runaway slaves via the Underground Railroad that extended through the southern tier of the state's counties.[9] In June 1848, a convention gathered in Buffalo, New York, to select a ticket for the fall election. This "Free Soil Party" nominated Charles C. Foote of Michigan as candidate for the vice presidency of the United States.[10] Support for their ticket siphoned votes from Cass's run for the presidency.

Such differences were temporarily laid aside when Michigan troops marched off to service in the Mexican War. None saw combat, and the number involved was relatively small. Afterward, a veteran of the conflict moved to Michigan in April 1849. "I was ordered to Detroit, Michigan, where two years were spent with but few important incidents."[11] The young officer spent the time in a house quite nice for its day and of which he must have been particularly fond. Married less than a year earlier, here is where he brought his new bride, Julia, for their first extended time together. The couple's first child, Fred, was born in Detroit on May 30, 1850. The clapboard-sided Greek Revival home with its adjacent grape arbor and garden were located on East Fort Street near the city center.[12] The officer's name would later be known to every American: Ulysses Simpson Grant.[13]

The Mexican War and its aftermath only exacerbated the slavery problem. A Michigan gathering[14] of some fifteen hundred people disgruntled over the then dominant Democratic and Whig political machines changed the course of history.

> By this time the people of Michigan were concerned with a problem that was every day more widely splitting the people of the United States. This was the problem of slavery…
>
> Those who were opposed to slavery were dissatisfied with the old political parties. In 1854 a group of anti-slavery people called a

meeting at Jackson, Michigan, to establish a new political party in which they felt they could have confidence.

So many people came to Jackson that there was no building large enough to hold the crowd. They met outdoors in what has been called the "Convention Under the Oaks" and chose the name Republican for their party. Several states claim to have been the birthplace of the national Republican party. Among these, Michigan has one of the strongest claims because of the convention at Jackson on July 6, 1854.

Michigan has an even firmer position in the beginning of the Republican party because of the election of 1854. Michigan's Republicans won the election, and Michigan was the first state to have a Republican governor, Kingsley Bingham. The Republicans also won three of the four seats in the United States House of Representatives, as well as both houses of the state legislature.[15]

Born in New York State in 1808, Bingham opposed extension of slavery into the western territories of Kansas and Nebraska and, after serving in the same Congress as Lincoln, left the Democratic Party for the party of freedom. He was reelected as governor in 1856.

That year also meant a presidential election. Stumping for Republican nominee John C. Fremont, a former congressman from Illinois came to an August rally in Kalamazoo. Abraham Lincoln's speech in Bronson Park did not excite reporters or many in attendance. His appearance suffered from the competing attractions: a giant "concourse" with a "free public table," parades, eight bands and the Battle Creek Glee Club. Plus, four speakers' stands were going simultaneously during the afternoon, so that the *Detroit Daily Advertiser* would lament it could assign only a single stenographic reporter to the speeches and added, "Our reporter stuck to the main stand." Lincoln was preceded by remarks from Zachariah Chandler of Detroit and then introduced by Hezekiah G. Wells of the Republican executive committee.

This is partly what Lincoln said:

This government is sought to be put on a new track. Slavery is to be made a ruling element in our government. The question can be avoided in but two ways. By the one, we must submit, and allow

MASS MEETING!

AT MASON, SEPT. 9th, 1854.

To the People of Ingham County, without distinction of Party:

In view of the recent action of Congress in regard to the organization of Nebraska and Kansas Territories, and the evident designs of the Slave power to attempt still further aggressions upon Freedom, we invite all our Fellow Citizens, without reference to former political associations, who think that the time has arrived for a Union at the North, to protect Liberty from being overthrown and down-trodden, to assemble in

Mass Convention,

On Saturday, the 9th day of September next, at 10 o'clock A. M., at the Court House, in the Village of Mason, for the purpose of putting in nomination suitable persons to fill the County offices, Representative to the State Legislature, delegates to the Congressional and Senatorial Conventions, and to transact such other business as may be deemed expedient.

D. G. McClure, J. W. Holmes, W. Jones, Geo. W. Dart, R. Foster, W. Foster, C. O. Stiles, G. A. Brown, J. W. Soule, A. W. Williams, H A. Rueght, D. M. Bagley, M. K. North, H. Bisby, J. O. Smith, C. Thomas, H. H. North, Roswell Everitt, O. D. Skinner, Joshua North, H. Lester, F. R. West, J. Paul, M. T Hicks, R Stephens, W° M Stephens, H. D. Granger, J. D. Reeves, A. P. Hicks, A. H. Roble, S. S. Green, C. E. Royce, David Hale, R. Howell, K. Johnson, J. N. Bush, H. Baker, H. L. Baker, J P. Powell, O. D. Parker, E. C. Barker, S. Lovell, J. H. Lobdell, J. W. Demerest, W. S. Calkins, James I. Mead, J. Robson, L. D. Quackimbush, F. N. Grilley, S. A. Tooker, A. Nois, S. Harrington, A. Cline, S Sanderson, S Dunn, J W Phelps, John Dunsbach, Jr., Sanford Marsh, Geo Smith, Levi Buck, Geo Chappell, Z L Holmes, Thos Treat, C White, H Bristol, W H Child, H Converss S R Wilcox, S Crosman, S B Wessels, N Parks, J W Ball, Wm Tanner, D J Cobb, E F Thompson, N Brace, A Olds, Wm Baldwin, I. Merrill, L H Spencer, W F Lindsey, E V Van Epps, E W Cooledge, W B Hildreth, T Lester, R W Burdick J T Irish, S Heth, J E North, J North, S Barton, S R Greene, Wm Lee, W H Pinckney, H B Shank, O B Webster, S D Newbro, E P Newbro, J H Rowley, A B Bagley, N C Branch, U M Chappell, C C Darling, John G Darling, W. E. Everitt.

August 30th, 1854.

A broadside announces a mass meeting in Mason on September 9, 1854, to oppose "the Slave power."

slavery to triumph, or, by the other, we must triumph over the black demon. We have chosen the latter manner. If you of the North wish to get rid of this question, you must decide between these two ways—submit and vote for Buchanan, submit and vote that slavery is a just and good thing and immediately get rid of the question; or unite with us, and help us to triumph. We would all like to have the question done away with, but we cannot submit.

The nation decided, and James Buchanan won. His fellow Michigan Democrat, Lewis Cass, espoused their party's political philosophy, which was quite different from the one held by Lincoln and his fellow Republicans. They held that the people of a territory ought to decide whether to authorize or prohibit slavery. Cass had risen to the top post in his party in Michigan, having served as territorial governor, U.S. secretary of war, U.S. senator, ambassador and presidential candidate in 1848. Buchanan named him secretary of state.

Two years later, the Michigan governorship was again on the line. Competing for the post were Democrat Charles P. Stuart and Republican Moses Wisner. Securing his law license in 1841, Wisner began practicing in Lapeer as prosecuting attorney thanks to an appointment by Governor William Woodbridge, a Whig. An abolitionist, Wisner participated in the 1854 gathering under the oaks in Jackson. His success as an attorney in Oakland County, exemplified by accumulation of almost six thousand acres of land, pushed him to prominence and led to nomination in the gubernatorial election in '58. Running as a Republican to replace the state's first governor from that party, Wisner beat Stuart, one of the sitting U.S. senators, by over nine thousand votes.[16]

As Republicans solidified their hold on Michigan, slavery opponents came from other states to seek support. On March 12, 1859, abolitionist John Brown of Kansas met with a number of prominent African Americans in a house in the heart of Detroit. A non-Michigander also attended by the name of Frederick Douglass. In this historic interracial meeting, Brown sought their assistance for an urgent, violent plan against slavery. Douglass and the Detroiters opposed the approach.[17] Seven months later, Brown and a small cadre of followers stormed and briefly held the federal arsenal at Harpers Ferry, Virginia. The slave uprising he sought to foment did not occur, and Brown was captured and hanged.

The state of Michigan was but twenty-three years old when it participated in the momentous 1860 election. Inhabited by nearly 750,000 free persons, Michigan ranked sixteenth in the nation and ninth out of the twenty-two Northern states in population.[18] That year, Lincoln captured the Republican nomination for president and ran on a platform opposing the extension of slavery.[19] He did not visit Michigan during the campaign, as was customary for candidates; William Seward of New York did stump for Lincoln[20] in the state and received enthusiastic welcomes.[21] Lincoln won; in Michigan, he took

88,445 votes compared to 64,958 for second-place finisher Stephen Douglas, the Northern Democratic candidate. In the country as a whole, Lincoln received 180 electoral votes, while his competitors received a combined total of 123. All 6 of Michigan's electoral votes went in the Lincoln column,[22] aiding his elevation to the White House.

The election outcome prompted South Carolina to bolt the Union the next month.[23] A week before the Southerners' decision, Lewis Cass resigned from the Buchanan cabinet, complaining that the administration was too "doughface" in the crisis that was daily escalating.[24] It had not mobilized the Federal military or taken strong action to protect U.S. property. Cass was convinced that forceful action would have faced down Southerners who were threatening secession.[25] His sentiments were echoed by other Michiganders, who watched as Southern states that had helped keep theirs out of the Union were now attempting to destroy what it had fought so hard to enter.[26]

Governor Wisner's final address[27] to the legislature in early 1861 did not mince words: "This is no time for vacillating councils when the cry of treason is ringing in our ears. The constitution as our fathers made it, is good enough for us, and must be enforced upon every foot of American soil."[28] On January 8, 1861, a salute of one hundred guns was fired in Detroit to honor the defense of Charleston Harbor when the garrison moved to Fort Sumter.[29] On March 15, the legislature authorized Governor Austin Blair—another Republican—to supply troops to aid the federal government. News of the firing on Fort Sumter was received the same day it occurred, thanks to the telegraph. The thunderbolt shock of war that April Sunday when the fort surrendered found Michigan unprepared for the news—but the shock did not immobilize it.

Recall the great seal of the state of Michigan. In addition to bearing a date representing its fight to get into the Union, the seal featured an eagle, symbolic of the national bird, with yet another message, the phrase "E Pluribus Unum": from out of many, one. Michigan had embraced the Revolutionary War–era motto, also found on the Federal seal, portraying that out of many colonies—or states—emerged a single nation, indivisible. And that is where Michigan came down as the nation's flag was being lowered at Fort Sumter.

Chapter 3

ANSWERING LINCOLN'S CALL

To say that Michigan performed her whole duty in her efforts to aid in suppressing the rebellion would not be saying enough; for, considering the low ebb of her finances at the time, it was an undertaking under great disadvantage, and especially so as Michigan, like most of the other States, had in the past made but a very feeble preparation, in a military point of view, to meet an emergency of that magnitude.[30]

The surrender of Fort Sumter prompted President Lincoln to call on loyal states for seventy-five thousand volunteers to put down the rebellion. It constituted a huge order. Michigan's military force consisted of twenty-eight militia companies of 1,240 men. They were not organized into regiments or supported by sufficient public funds, since the state appropriation equaled just $3,000. Each company had to pay its own way; most were poorly equipped, all were poorly armed. In August the year before, the first-ever state encampment had met in Jackson under the direction of militia veteran Alpheus Williams of Detroit. It proved useful when the war started but hardly furnished a ready response.[31]

The antebellum legislature had been unmoved by arguments for bolstering the military:[32] "Michigan, in common with other Northern States, had shared in the prevailing indifference" as to the prospect of armed conflict. "Thus the times of peace had not been devoted to a preparation for war."[33] In March 1861, while Fort Sumter effectively was under siege, an "act to provide a military force" was passed providing for recruitment of enough soldiers to form two regiments. They could drill up to ten days per month. One legislator, a former governor, sought to amend the bill by inserting "corn"—not referring to foodstuffs but to military leadership, i.e., "corn field officers." No appropriations followed, and no implementation transpired.[34]

First responses to Fort Sumter were from ordinary civilians. When news arrived of the attack on April 13, lawyers in Detroit quickly convened at the bar library to avow their fealty to the Union. A day after the surrender, a Union meeting was held at the Firemen's Hall. Lincoln's call for troops was issued on April 15; the next day, Governor Blair responded with a trip to Detroit from Lansing, where he issued an immediate call for a regiment of ten companies. At a meeting later that day, when fulfilling Michigan's quota would likely require $100,000, Detroit's citizens pledged a loan of half that amount. "The amounts thus raised, as well as all other indebtedness incurred in like manner, were assumed by the State on the assembling of the Legislature."[35]

Each succeeding day saw more mobilization, more *esprit*. At an April 17 ceremony, the American flag was ceremonially raised over the Detroit Board of Trade building and speeches were given in support of the Union; "General" Cass was present, lending his support. The Detroit Light Guards met up to organize for war service. On April 18, the flag was raised on top of the custom house and post office to confirm the security of Federal installations in the state. On April 20, a ceremony was held in front of the post office and an oath of loyalty administered to all government officials. The Sherlock, Scott and Brady Guards organized in anticipation of being called up. On April 23, the flag was again raised in a ceremony at Firemen's Hall, and on April 25, it was flown over the city hall for a pro-Union speech by Cass and the singing of the "Star-Spangled Banner" by three thousand school children.

The War Department implemented Lincoln's decree by assigning quotas to the various loyal states. Despite remonstrances by Governor Austin Blair that Michigan could furnish more, it was initially called upon to supply just a single infantry regiment. On May 4, the legislature made provision for relief of the families of volunteers who would respond.[36] Many did, and the First Michigan Infantry was formed largely out of militia companies in Adrian, Ann Arbor, Burr Oak, Coldwater, Detroit, Jackson, Manchester, Marshall and Ypsilanti. On May 11 came a formal presentation of banner and cockades to the troop at Campus Martius. Two days later, the regiment left for the nation's capital

An oath of allegiance is said on April 20, 1861, before the old Detroit post office on Griswold, south of the first capitol.

under the command of Colonel Orlando Willcox of Detroit, appointed by Blair to head Michigan's first responders.

Once the scales had fallen from its eyes, and the War Department increased its allotment, Michigan was springing into action. On June 2, the Second Michigan Infantry left the city. Many more soldiers in many other units would follow their path. The War Department designated Fort Wayne in Detroit as a camp of instruction from which many of Michigan's troops were mustered, trained and dispatched to the front.

> *The emergencies and duties of the hour were then fully realized by the people of the State, and the uprising was universal...pledging fidelity and pecuniary assistance to the Nation in its hour of great peril, and volunteers in large numbers were congregating and demanding instant service for the Union, while the watch-fires of patriotism had been kindled on every hillside and in every*

First Michigan Infantry receives a flag from "the Ladies & Citizens of Detroit" on May 11, 1861.

valley, burning and flashing with intense brightness, at once cheering and inspiring.[37]

The trustees of Adrian College offered the use of campus buildings and grounds to the Fourth Infantry for training, a site named Camp Williams. The City of Adrian donated money to build a mess and dining hall. By early June, ten companies of the Fourth had arrived and started their training. On June 21, nearly thirty thousand people came to see them off to Washington. The women of Adrian presented the unit with a regimental flag bearing this admonition: "The Ladies of Adrian to the Fourth regiment Defend It."

The Third Infantry marches down Detroit's Jefferson Avenue in the June 6, 1861 edition of the *New-York Illustrated News*.

Similar events took place at Camp Owen in Marshall and other camps around the state. Not all found the traditional three branches appropriate to their skills. Over in Illinois, a regiment of engineers was being raised, and advertisements went out to neighboring states. In Michigan, with even more infantry companies being raised than the War Department had authorized, some saw the Illinois opportunity as their chance to serve. By end of summer, companies of engineers were forming in five Michigan communities to head to Chicago. Then, on September 10, four Grand Rapids businessmen met.

Surveyor Wright Coffinberry, master carpenter Baker Borden, merchant James Sligh and contractor Perrin Fox "decided that it would be better to raise an entire engineer regiment within the state and 'thereby give Michigan the credit' than to send companies elsewhere." After securing the war secretary's sign off on September 11, the four telegraphed the governor for his approval. Blair jumped on a train for Grand Rapids the night he received the telegram, met with the four on the morning of the twelfth and gave his approval so long as the regiment would be known as the First Michigan Engineers and Mechanics. He telegraphed the secretary on the thirteenth of having "cheerfully authorized" the regiment. Adjutant General John Robertson issued General

Order No. 76 on the same day, announcing the regiment's formation. Four days is all it took to secure Michigan its most unique unit.[38]

Such support was not unusual. The First Michigan Infantry went off to war well organized: "Michigan sent off her first regiment fully armed, well equipped, fairly well drilled and in condition to at once take the field. It was ready to leave the state, and importuning for orders to do so, before those orders came."[39]

They arrived in Baltimore on May 16 where, not long before, a Massachusetts regiment had been attacked by Southern sympathizers. The mob "was still there, but it did not venture to raise its hand against the Michigan soldiers."[40] The regiment safely went on to D.C. Arriving in the nation's capital was exhilarating. The *New York Tribune* reported: "No regiment that has yet arrived has created such an excitement as the Michigan First."[41] An enthusiastic crowd came out to welcome the Michiganders, though it was 10:00 p.m., for they were "the first western regiment which had arrived at the capital."[42] Proceeding to the White House on the second day after arriving, the officers and band serenaded the president, were invited into the East Room and exchanged greetings.[43]

Michigan troops struck quite the image. One historian writes of how its earliest regiments were "formed of the hardiest of the state's youth."[44] "These rowdy Michiganders would earn a reputation as being among the most ferocious fighters of the war, perhaps because of their rugged frontier background."[45] They did not have to wait long.

At 2:00 a.m. on May 24, the First Michigan went into action. Crossing the Potomac River on the Long Bridge, it stepped onto Rebel-held Virginia, a move that "was historic as the opening aggressive movement—the entry of the Grand Army of the Republic, as it was then named for the first time, upon the sacred soil."[46] It marched down to Alexandria to take back the city, cooperating with a regiment of New Yorkers. Their commander, Elmer Ellsworth, an associate of the president, was killed hauling down the Confederate flag from above a hotel. The Rebel troops fled at the appearance of the Michiganders, and Willcox had the honor of reclaiming the town by raising "the Stars and Stripes over the captured city."[47]

Would the fortunes of war continue to smile on the regiment? At first, yes, as Willcox's talent was rewarded with larger brigade command. The Union army prepared to advance on the Rebel force near Manassas Junction, Virginia, beyond a tributary called Bull Run. On July 21, the armies clashed as the

The advance of the "Michigan regiment" into Alexandria in the May 24, 1861 edition of *Harper's Weekly.*

Federals swept across the creek and around the left wing of the Southerners, initially gaining the upper hand. Willcox's brigade came in on the far right of the Federal line. In the see-saw affair in that sector, the First Michigan advanced during a key moment to retake a battery of artillery that had fallen into Rebel hands. The regiment marched across fields and down the right side of Sudley Road, coming in at an opportune moment and rescuing the guns. Opening fire from the fence along the road, the left of the regiment drove off the Confederates and advanced to the point of woods south of the Henry House. The plan was to get into the Rebel rear and cause much mischief. But Willcox's horse was hit, as was he in the right forearm. Captain William Withington of Jackson came up and led his commander into the woods, where he dismounted and attempted a return to the Union lines. A captain of a Virginia regiment confronted the two and took them prisoner.

Also engaged in the battle were the Second and Third Michigan in the brigade commanded by General Israel Richardson of Pontiac and the Fourth Michigan in Willcox's. Richardson's troops fought their way across Bull Run and to a position opposite the Henry House, where they exchanged fire with Stonewall Jackson's troops. The Fourth Michigan was on detached service at Fairfax Court House. Willcox's after-action report noted that his old regiment

Left: Medal of Honor winner William Withington.

Below: The return of the three-months' regiment. Lewis Cass spoke at this event.

"deserves the credit of advancing farther into the enemy's lines than any other of our troops," as their dead on the field proved.

The fortitude of Michiganders was not cooled after the defeat and Willcox's capture. The example of the four regiments helped spur continuing enlistments.[48] As fall came on and the nation faced the reality that defeating the rebellion would require a long and hard war, Michigan men continued to be mustered into Federal service. "During the first year of fighting, twenty-one Michigan regiments were formed. Michigan men fought in most of the early battles of the war in the East."[49]

Michigan was answering the call, and its efforts on behalf of the Union cause were not flagging.

Chapter 4

1862: Swings of the Pendulum

The calendar page on the first year of the war had been turned. The first major battle at Bull Run had seen Michigan lose approximately one hundred men killed, wounded and missing or captured. The losses were chiefly from one regiment. Two others had covered the Union army's retreat from the battleground and were the absolute final line of protection for the Federal troops. The second year of the war would prove to be one of much greater cost.[50]

In the spring, Ulysses S. Grant, now a general, was in command of an army in middle Tennessee readying itself for continuing the offensive he had embarked upon in February. After capturing Forts Henry and Donelson near the Kentucky border, Grant had moved down the Tennessee River toward a Rebel army at Corinth, Mississippi. The town was a march away of a day or so from his base at Pittsburg Landing. Early on the morning of April 6, 1862, the Confederates sprang upon Grant's troops while they were still encamped. The Federals gave ground until a line of defense was constructed back at the landing, halting the Rebels after a daylong struggle. With the protection of nightfall, the Northerners regrouped. Reinforcements crossed the river to Grant, and the next day, his troops pushed the Confederates back past the Union campsites and into retreat. It was a battle known by the name of a rural church building near one of those camps—Shiloh—and it was a bloodbath.

Combined, the two armies suffered over twenty thousand casualties, far in excess of anything experienced in the war to this point. Grant's force lost over thirteen thousand. Michigan troops—the Twelfth, Thirteenth and Fifteenth Regiments—were among those bloodied. The Twelfth was a component

The Free Press.

EXTRA.

MONDAY, FEB. 17—12 M.

FORT DONELSON TAKEN.

TWELVE THOUSAND PRISONERS.

Reported Escape of Floyd, Buckner and Pillow.

Dispatch to the Michigan Exchange.
CHICAGO, Feb. 17.
Fort Donelson taken with twelve thousand prisoners, (12,000.)

Second Dispatch.
Dispatch to R. N. Rice, Esq.
CHICAGO, Feb. 17—11:45 A. M.
I suppose you have the glorious news of the surrend r of Fort Donelson.

The only drawback is the reported escape of Floyd, Pillow, Buckner and Johnson.

The surrender of the fort with its armament and fifteen thousand (15,000) prisoners however is glory enough for one day.

The city is wild with delight. Flags are up everywhere, but there is great anxiety for particulars.

Our Illinois troops were largely engaged and Chicago strongly represented represented by Taylor's Battery.

H. E. SARGENT.

Detroit Free Press screams "Extra" on Monday, February 17, 1862, about the capture of Fort Donelson and twelve thousand prisoners.

of the Sixth Division, under the command of Brigadier General Benjamin Prentiss, and of the First Brigade, commanded by Lieutenant Colonel William H. Graves, of Adrian, who had been wounded at First Bull Run. The regiment was camped in the Union center at the tip of the spear in the position farthest toward the Confederates at Corinth. On the evening before the Rebel attack, Graves—still smarting from the defeat in the east—took it upon himself to order one company to reconnoiter into the woods ahead. Around 8:30 p.m., its captain reported back that long lines of campfires stretched out to his front, right and left. The report was passed up to Prentiss, who dismissed it, but Graves's commanding officer thought different: he ordered a contingent, including two companies of the Twelfth, out in front as a trip wire in case an attack was imminent. The Rebels fell upon this advance picket at 3:00 a.m., and the great battle commenced. The Twelfth fought on during the day as part of three successive lines of defense, until the division was surrounded and many of its number captured. Prentiss was among those taken as prisoners. The Twelfth suffered over two hundred casualties.

The Fifteenth Infantry arrived at the landing on April 5, the day before the battle, and encamped. Lacking ammunition, it nonetheless advanced to the sound of battle the next morning. At first, it went into the fight with bayonets only, but after securing ammunition in the rear, returned to the action, losing over one hundred men. Such Michigan infantrymen were not the only units engaged. Battery B of the First Light Artillery fought at the Peach Orchard and near a pool that became known as the Bloody Pond. It stood its ground in the face of several charges but finally was overcome by superior numbers. Losing four of its six guns, half of the First's men were also captured. Michigan's soldiers had helped hold back the Confederate advance long enough for Grant to construct his line of defense, paving the way for victory.[51]

Back East, a new commander had a new plan to advance on Richmond to take the capital of the Confederacy and end the war in one fell swoop. In March 1862, General George McClellan transported most of his Army of the Potomac down that river to the peninsula between the James and York Rivers, anchored by a base of operations at Fortress Monroe on its eastern tip. Another wing remained between the two cities to protect Washington. In April, the Union force began cautiously moving toward Richmond. Not until early May did the first significant encounter result at Williamsburg. The Second Infantry went into action after a trying march, losing several officers and some sixty men in total. In one account of that fighting, a private who had received his weapon only the day before was found on the field beside a dead Confederate, both transfixed by the other's bayonet. A young lieutenant from Michigan led a small detachment in an assault on a Confederate redoubt. It was the first real experience under fire for George A. Custer of Monroe, and his intrepid leadership earned him favorable mention in his commander's battle report. The fighting near the colonial capital forced the Rebels back into the outskirts of Richmond.

Confederate commander Joseph Johnston developed a plan to drive the Union army away, but the Battle of Fair Oaks in early June resulted in his severe wounding and no favorable outcome, except for appointment of his replacement, Robert E. Lee. The new commander of the Army of Northern

John Braden, Fifth Infantry (Detroit), was wounded at Williamsburg, Gettysburg and Locust Grove, Virginia. He was discharged at expiration of service in October 1864.

Virginia would become the Confederate general whom the Michigan units would confront in the East over the next several years. In a near-continuous fight known as the Seven Days Battles during the last week in June and on July 1, Lee took the offensive and drove McClellan away from Richmond. When the smoke finally cleared on the week's fighting, over thirty-five thousand soldiers were casualties. Michigan troops had fought well,[52] including an artillery commander born in Michigan during a key point that saved his army.

The Army of the Potomac had its back to the James River with Lee closing in. Nearby, on a sloping plateau known as Malvern Hill, a long line of cannons was placed in front of the blue infantry. As the gray lines moved into position, Detroiter Henry Jackson Hunt double-checked the position of his hundred guns. They opened up on the Confederate infantry units, as each attacked.

John Emory Crane, First Infantry (Hillsdale County), son of a Pioneer Wesleyan minister, died of disease in a hospital at Fort Monroe on July 4, 1862.

When Rebel artillery attempted piecemeal counter fire, the Union batteries knocked them out of action one by one. The day was a disaster for Lee and became forever known for the central role played by the Federal cannons without serious infantry support. Hunt had so capably organized and managed the artillery here, defeating Lee. They would meet in similar circumstances a year later in Pennsylvania.

McClellan sought to reinforce and resupply his Army of the Potomac before resuming any forward movement. Lee took the opportunity to move his army back toward northern Virginia and require McClellan to follow. In late August, opposing forces met again on the battleground near Manassas.[53] Lee dispatched one of his army's wings under Stonewall Jackson to attack the Union line of supply, after which Jackson went into defensive mode to lure the Union troops into battle. The trap worked, and when Lee's other wing arrived they smashed into the unprotected Federal left flank. The result was total collapse and retreat by the Union force.

Once again, a rear guard action on the road to Washington became necessary to save the United States army from destruction at Manassas. Federal cavalry came to the rescue. General John Buford, later of Gettysburg renown, shouted, "Boys, save our army, cover their retreat," and the First Michigan Cavalry charged into the pursuing Confederates. The tactic succeeded, but at a high price. The colonel of the First Cavalry, Thornton Fleming Brodhead of Grosse Ile, was mortally wounded.[54]

During the fighting on the second day at Manassas, Michigan infantry was in place on both ends of the line. The Third Michigan held the right, and the First and Sixteenth were on the left. The latter two regiments were engaged in the assault on Jackson, crossing the field near Groveton under heavy artillery fire. As they attacked Stonewall's brigades head-on, they became exposed to the flank attack. The Sixteenth was much cut up; the First, in a matter of minutes, lost eight officers and half of the regiment. Neither had anything to show for their courage under fire except combat laurels.

Lee continued as the aggressor. After Second Bull Run, he launched an invasion into Maryland, hoping to enlist sympathizers to the Southern side and European nations to recognize the legitimacy of the Confederacy. Splitting his army into several elements to collect provisions and recruits, he deployed several units as a screen in the mountain passes on his eastern flank to prevent McClellan from using them to attack before the separated fragments could reunite. On September 14, the Army of the Potomac sought to force the passes. The Seventeenth Infantry went into action at South Mountain; at midday, Confederate artillery opened up on the regiment as it supported the Union guns. After enduring the shelling for several hours, the regiment finally was ordered to attack the Rebels in the looming dusk. Their task was a daunting one: the enemy was posted behind stone walls at the top of the hill. Advancing up the mountain under heavy fire, the green regiment carried the Rebel defenses and drove the enemy back down the other side of the crest. The way was clear for McClellan to go after Lee. The regiment lost a third of their number but gained a nickname for its indomitable feat as the "Stonewall Regiment."[55] Its commander: Colonel William Withington, who was finally exchanged after his capture at First Bull Run.

John A. Clark, Seventh Infantry (Monroe), held the ranks of sergeant, second lieutenant and first lieutenant. He was killed in action at Antietam on September 17, 1862.

McClellan attacked Lee near Sharpsburg, Maryland, along Antietam Creek.[56] He did so, however, in stages, allowing the Confederates to mount successive defensive lines. The Seventh Michigan went into action on the right of the Union line in the West Woods, under the command of Norman Hall of Fort Sumter fame. More than half the force engaged was disabled. Officers killed in this action were James Turrill of Lapeer, John Eberhard of Burr Oak and John A. Clark and Allen Zacharias of Monroe.

In the center, Major General Richardson led his division in an advance across open fields to a sunken road where Confederates lay in wait. The Federals were cut down in swaths. Richardson continued the attacks on this Bloody Lane until the Rebels were driven off with heavy casualties of their own—and until he was shot down. Taken to the rear, Richardson died several days after the battle.

After the success in the center, the left wing of McClellan's army captured a bridge across the creek, enabling an advance on the remaining thin line of

Confederates toward the close of the day's action. Orlando Willcox advanced here on the left with a force that included the Eighth Michigan Infantry. He was pressing the Confederates back and nearing the town of Sharpsburg when ordered to withdraw. He would later wonder what might have happened if allowed to press his advance. The bloodiest day in American military history had ended. Some 350 Michiganders were killed or wounded, including the death of the highest ranking officer it sent to war.

Out in the western theater, opposing armies under Confederate Braxton Bragg and Union general William Rosecrans met at Perryville, Kentucky, in October. Both were searching for suitable supplies of drinking water during a particularly hot fall. Bragg attacked part of Rosecrans's army with nearly all of his but, in a battle that could have gone against the Federals, it ended up withdrawing. Battery A of the First Light Artillery under Cyrus Loomis of Coldwater played an important role. It was reported to have fired both the first and last shots of the day's action. It fought a lengthy duel with the Washington Artillery of the Confederate side; it repelled five charges; and it claimed to have saved the Union right flank. The battery suffered eighteen casualties and lost thirty-three horses.[57]

The year ended in disaster for the Army of the Potomac. In December, it stole a march on Lee's army, but a logistics failure prevented pontoon boats

"Camp of 16th Michigan Regiment near Fredricksburg [sic]," a lithograph by A. Hoen & Co., Baltimore, December 13, 1862.

from arriving across from the town of Fredericksburg when the army could have marched into the town and onto the heights beyond. By the time bridge-building apparatus was on the scene, so was Lee. Attempts to force a landing were thwarted by sharpshooters firing at the Federal bridge builders from hidden locations in houses and structures in the town.

At first, Union infantry units were moved into position to provide cover for the engineers. When that proved ineffective, volunteers were sought to cross the river and eliminate the Rebel snipers. Henry Baxter of Jonesville, colonel of the Seventh Michigan—at the request of his brigade commander, Colonel Hall—agreed to storm the town.

Hall's after action account is thus:

> *I stated to Colonel Baxter that I saw no hopes of effecting the crossing, unless he could man the oars, place the boats, and push across unassisted. I confess I felt apprehensions of disaster in this attempt, as, without experience in the management of boats, the shore might not be reached promptly, if at all, and the party lost. Colonel Baxter promptly accepted the new conditions, and proceeded immediately to arrange the boats, some of which had to be carried to the water...The boats pushed gallantly across under a sharp fire. While in the boats, 1 man was killed and Lieutenant Colonel Baxter and several men were wounded. The party, which numbered from 60 to 70 men, formed under the bank and rushed upon the first street, attacked the enemy, and, in the space of a few minutes, 31 prisoners were captured and a secure lodgment effected. Several men were here also wounded, and Lieutenant Emery and 1 man killed. The remainder of the regiment meanwhile crossed.*

The one fatality was Lieutenant Franklin Emery of Lapeer.

According to later accounts, the Michigan troops included Robert Henry Hendershot, who became known as "the Drummer Boy of the Rappahannock." Like Michigander Charles Gardner, he was a drummer for the Eighth Michigan. His regiment was stationed near the Seventh, and when it was crossing the Rappahannock under fire, it was said that young Robert ran to help push the boats. He had crossed the river when a shell fragment hit his drum and broke it into pieces; picking up a musket, he encountered

George W. Curtis, First Infantry (Houghton County), enlisted at age thirty in July 1861, reenlisted February 17, 1864, and was wounded in action on March 29, 1865.

a Confederate soldier and took him prisoner. The story of a boy capturing a Rebel made him a hero.[58]

During assaults on Confederate positions beyond the town, much of the Michigan infantry was held in reserve. The First again was called upon to participate in an assault with little chance of success. They suffered losses while forming for the assault in town and then took more casualties as they tried to take the heights. Captain J. Benton Kennedy of Jackson was mortally wounded while leading his company. Remaining on the field until dark, the regiment was not withdrawn until late the following day. The experience of the Fourth Michigan was much the same: being ordered into action, left on the field overnight and withdrawn after the loss of a number of enlisted men and Lieutenant James Clark of Ann Arbor. Covering the assaults was the artillery fire from across the river of Henry Hunt.[59]

The very end of the year brought about an unusual action. At the Battle of Stones River near Murfreesboro, Tennessee, armies under Rosecrans and Bragg fought on December 31, 1862, and New Year's Day 1863. Both commanders planned an attack on the other's right. After the two days, Rosecrans claimed victory when Bragg withdrew. It would take over a century for commemoration of the role played by Michigan soldiers in a number of units during the battle. The text of the 1966 monument revealed that the marker is

dedicated to all the Michigan soldiers engaged in this great battle, to the seventy-one men who lost their lives and to the six regiments which fought bravely for their country: Twenty-first Michigan Infantry, commanded by Lieutenant Colonel William B. McCreery (Flint), 18 killed, 89 wounded, 36 missing; Eleventh Michigan Infantry, commanded by Colonel William Stoughton (Sturgis), 30 killed, 84 wounded, 25 missing; Thirteenth Michigan Infantry,

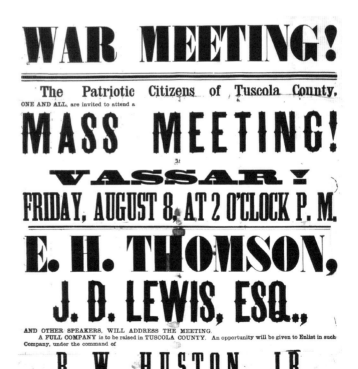

A Tuscola County "Mass War Meeting" is announced on July 28, 1862.

commanded by Colonel Michael Shoemaker (Jackson), 17 killed, 72 wounded; Fourth Michigan Cavalry, commanded by Colonel Robert H.G. Minty (Detroit), 1 killed, 7 wounded, 12 missing; First Michigan Engineers and Mechanics, commanded by Colonel William P. Innes (Grand Rapids), 2 killed, 9 wounded, 5 missing; First Michigan Artillery Battery, Company A, commanded by Colonel Cyrus O. Loomis (Coldwater), 1 killed, 10 wounded, 2 missing. Michigan men fought at Stones River for the preservation and perpetuity of the Union.

The year closed with significant Union victories out West—despite missteps—and no significant change in affairs in the East. The casualties had mounted far beyond expectations; huge portions of Confederate territory were in Union hands, but the Rebel capital remained defiant. Warfare during 1862 did produce one seismic shift: after the Battle of Antietam, Lincoln announced that, on the first of the new year, he would issue a proclamation freeing all slaves within Confederate territory. On the same winter's day, Michigan troops were fighting along a river in central Tennessee when Lincoln inked his name to the war measure that achieved liberty for millions of Americans in the rest of the South. The Emancipation Proclamation was celebrated by many in Michigan, including its Republican leadership.

The war was continuing, but America would never be the same.

Chapter 5

WOMEN OF WAR

Spies and nurses: that's what most have heard of the role of women in the Civil War. The picture for Michigan's contingent is painted on a larger and more colorful canvas. The role women played in the antebellum antislavery movement in Michigan, from surreptitious assistance on the Underground Railroad to open advocacy of abolition, must be acknowledged first. Before statehood, Elizabeth Margaret Chandler at age twenty-three organized the Logan Female Anti-Slavery Society in Lenawee County and published abolitionist poems. Laura Smith Haviland aided Chandler's efforts and, after her friend's death, founded the Raisin Institute, the first school in Michigan to admit African Americans. This contingent of freedom fighters was not lily white: Sojourner Truth of "Ain't I a Woman?" fame took up antebellum residence in Battle Creek.[60] On the prewar stage, Michigan's women played a large and important role.

Their contributions to liberty and equality only increased after the conflict was joined. Units were sent off to the field with flags conceived and stitched together by women of the community. On November 6, 1861, the nation's first "Ladies' Soldiers' Aid Society" organized in Detroit for the benefit of troops away at camps, in hospitals and on battlefields. The smoke from First Bull Run "had hardly disappeared before scores of Detroit ladies were busily engaged in scraping lint, and in collecting and preparing needed comforts for the sick and wounded."[61] Society members extended their services to soldiers' homes in Detroit and other Michigan locales, as well as to facilities such as the one Lincoln frequented in Washington during trips to his "summer White House."

As ninety thousand men marched away to war, women served in every capacity on the home front that society would permit. Precursors to World War II's Rosie the Riveter, some performed the jobs in which men were employed before enlistment. The leading occupations in 1860s Michigan were agrarian; with husbands gone as soldiers, wives assumed the responsibility to ensure that planting, nurturing and harvesting would occur. Although they did not enjoy equal property rights during this era, women effectively became copartners on farms all across the state. In filling this gap, women confronted challenges no one had prepared them to face: business decisions, financial choices, family care giving, loneliness, fear and anxiety. Isolation became all the more difficult because of the distance Michigan was from the two theaters of war and the difficulties of travel.

The birth of their child while her husband was absent—in a time when pregnancy could be life threatening—became even more of an ordeal. A typically evocative letter written nearing full term while the husband was away ends: "Oh how I wish you nere [sic] to come to the bed and talk to us once but as you can't do this I am thankful we can right [sic] to each other."[62] Letter author Nan Ewing would, later that same year, open a letter from her husband to discover he had lost an eye in combat near Petersburg, Virginia. She could do nothing but write back to him. Despite everything, Michigan women persevered.

War can bring momentous changes to the social order, and Civil War Michigan experienced this phenomenon. Not all women felt that duty required remaining at home. Some wives went to the front with their husbands, attempting to take care of them as they had when civilians. Some stayed at nearby havens, paying visits as frequently as military discipline permitted to offer encouragement and support. Some were permitted to stay in camp to serve as laundresses or matrons, helping the soldiers with domestic chores. And some did serve as medical personnel, working with the Sanitary Commission or the U.S. Christian Commission.[63]

The most dramatic development was the female in uniform. Some women attempted to join up, only to be discovered and discharged. Mary Burns disguised herself in order to enlist in the Seventh Michigan Cavalry. Before the regiment left Detroit, however, her gender was found out. Since she was in uniform, it prompted her arrest, imprisonment in the city jail and a charge of masquerading as a man.[64] The criminal code of the 1860s enforced the common assumption that women could not face hostile fire.

The most widely known female soldier's story is that of Private Franklin Thompson of Company F, Second Michigan Infantry, and an enlistee from Flint. In April 1863, Private Thompson deserted—or, more accurately, fled the ranks. The cause for flight was not fear of battle but of discovery, for Thompson was no ordinary man. He was, in fact, a woman,

> *and a good looking one at that. She succeeded in concealing her sex most admirably, serving in various campaigns and battles of the regiment as a soldier; often employed as a spy, going within the enemy's lines, sometimes absent for weeks, and is said to have furnished much valuable information. She remained with the regiment until...it is supposed she apprehended a disclosure of*

Sarah Emma Edmonds
Seelye.

her sex and deserted at Lebanon, Kentucky, but where she went remains a mystery.[65]

In May 1882, the mystery was solved. Sarah Emma Edmonson Seelye wrote the Michigan adjutant general, asking for a certificate of service—under Thompson's name—which was required to pursue a claim for a federal soldier's pension. Once it was ascertained that the claim was truthful, she approached the United States Congress for relief. On July 5, 1884, a private bill awarding her the pension was signed into law, confirming her claim to have served in the military.[66] In July 1886, a bill became law removing the charge of desertion from her military record. A century later, Michigan erected a historical marker in Flint with this text: "The Second Michigan saw action at the first Battle of Bull Run and, as part of the Army of the Potomac, at the Second Bull Run and Fredericksburg. Thompson performed all of the duties of a soldier including nurse and mail carrier. In 1863 he became ill, but was denied a furlough. To preserve his identity, he deserted." Whether Thompson/Edmondson really served as a spy may be fiction. But completely genuine was the warmth with which she was greeted at the October 1884 regimental reunion in Flint.[67] Her comrades accepted her as one of Michigan's own.

Lesser known is the story of a soldier in the Twenty-fifth Michigan Infantry. At the Battle of Tebbs Bend, Kentucky, occurring on the day after the Battle of Gettysburg and on the surrender of Vicksburg, one of the soldiers in the regiment was badly wounded. At the field hospital, the surgeon was shocked to find his patient was not a male and thus, for yet one more time, a young woman named Lizzie Compton, who had fought and received a wound on behalf of the Union. Unlike some female Civil War combat vets, Lizzie's story has not yielded a book about her exploits. Several of the works that treat the general subject of women in the war reference her.[68] She appears to have originally joined when only fourteen, serving with several units until she was wounded at Tebbs Bend while in the Michigan unit. She was then sixteen. According to one source,[69] she "enlisted in eight different Union regiments" only to be discovered each time, resulting in discharge. In "A Strange Story: 'Truth Stranger than Fiction'—Lizzie Compton, the Soldier Girl," a contemporaneous article attributed first to the *Rochester Union*, this account is given of a traveler's arrest:

She stated that she was about sixteen years of age, assuming that she had been correctly informed as to the date of her birth. Her parents died in her infancy, near Nashville, Tenn., and she was left, as too many children are, to the tender mercies of unfeeling wretches. She was put into the field to work at an early age, and was never taught any duties of the household. When a child she wore a frock—but really was never fully clad in the apparel of her sex. At the age of thirteen, when the rebellion commenced, she put on the clothes of a boy and worked about the steamboats on the Western rivers. At length she sought a place in the army as a bugler, on which instrument she soon excelled.

Lizzie has been eighteen months in the service and in seven or eight regiments. She got into the ranks by fraud—taking the place of some person who had passed muster and was discharged as soon as her sex was discovered. Among the regiments in which she served were the 79th New York, 17th and 28th Michigan, and the 2nd Minnesota. Her first engagement was at Mill Springs, and she relates minutely the details of the fall of Zollicoffer. She was captured with her company and paroled by the guerrilla Morgan near Gallatin, Tenn. She fought at Fort Donelson, Shiloh, and several other places in the West. Finally she went to the Army of the Potomac and got into the 79th New York. At the battle of Fredericksburg, early in July, she was wounded by a piece of shell in the side; and the surgeon discovered and disclosed her sex, which led to her dismissal after recovering in the hospital. Her secret was twice betrayed by surgeons. While in a Western regiment she undertook to ride a horse which none of her companions dare mount, and being without a saddle, she was thrown and injured, which led to betrayal.

This girl, familiar with the use of a musket, understands the manual perfectly, has performed picket and other duties of camp and field, and delights in the service. She recites camp incidents and scenes with the ardor of a youth of twelve, and longs to be with her old companions in arms. When asked if she had no fears, she replied that she was some "skeered" in the first battle, but never since, and she added that as she had done nothing to lead her to believe she would go to a bad place in the next world, she was not afraid to die.

Lizzie is five feet one inch in height, and weighs 155 pounds, and is of course of rather stout build. She has light hair, fair complexion, and in her half military suit with high boots, and pants tucked in the tops, she has the appearance of a rosy soldier boy of fifteen years. She carries with her a paper from the Chief of Police of Louisville, Mr. Priest, stating who she is, and commending her to the favor of the railroad superintendents. She came to this city a few days since, and went to New York to see Barnum, who had written to her. He was not then in the city, and after spending a day or two there, she became disgusted and started Westward. She arrived here without money, and sought to enlist to provide for herself. She was not discouraged at her failure. She declared that she could work at any business a boy could do, and would earn her living if permitted to do so. She was told that the statute forbade a woman wearing a man's clothing, and that she must abandon the practice. She would not promise to make a change—indeed she insisted that she would prefer any punishment—death even—rather than be compelled to act the part of a woman.

Bail was entered for the good behavior of the soldier girl, and she took the cars to go where, we know not. She will no doubt appear soon in some other locality.

A story to rival Annie Oakley's, yet the Michigan adjutant general's postwar report does not include her name in the record of service in any unit.

It remains difficult to verify the service of women in uniform. An example is "Michigan Bridget," a woman associated with the First Michigan Cavalry. Some accounts report that she remained with the unit throughout the war, others that she went into battle as well. A letter written in March 1865 reported a visit "in company with Miss Bridget Deavers, two large camps of dismounted cavalrymen lying along the James River, a few miles from City Point. Bridget—or, as the men call her, Biddy—has probably seen more hardship and danger than any other woman during the war."

Her experience apparently was at the front line:

She has been with the cavalry all the time, going out with them on their cavalry raids—always ready to succor the wounded on the field—often getting men off who, but for her, would be left to die, and, fearless of shell or bullet, among the last to leave.

Protected by officers and respected by privates, with her little sunburnt face, she makes her home in the saddle or the shelter-tent; often, indeed, sleeping in the open air without a tent, and by her courage and devotion "winning golden opinions from all sorts of people."[70]

A number of Michigan women merited special commendation, whatever the renown. Anna Blair Etheridge received the Kearny Cross for distinguished service with the Second and Third Michigan Infantry. The medal was awarded to those who had performed acts of extreme heroism in the face of the enemy. Etheridge was known to have ridden her horse onto battlefields to act as nurse to wounded Michiganders. She was buried in Arlington National Cemetery in 1913. Julia Susan Wheelock, by then Mrs. Porter Freeman, under an 1890 Act of Congress, was awarded a pension of twelve dollars per month "on account of disability resulting from disease contracted while serving as a

Anna Etheridge.

hospital nurse during the war of the rebellion." Wheelock left Ionia in 1862 to care for her brother after he was wounded at Chantilly, Virginia. Arriving to find him a battle fatality, she decided to remain with the Michigan Soldier's Relief Association alongside Elmina Brainard, a young Michigan woman who had also volunteered as a nurse. Contemporary newspapers called Wheelock "the Florence Nightingale of Michigan."

Some women, as shown, merited a pension for service in a Michigan regiment. For others, societal issues prevented them from receiving their just due. Their service is known only to God. One who deserved a different kind of recognition was Winifred Lee Brent. Under her married name of Mrs. Henry Lyster,[71] she penned the words in late 1862 to "Michigan, My Michigan," a musical piece commemorating the service of Michigan troops during the war. It would become an official state song. Recounting the scenes of the Peninsula Campaign ("from Yorktown on to Richmond's walls"), Shiloh, Antietam and Fredericksburg, the lyrics hail those fighting in battle and those at home whose pride in their servicemen was mingled with loss.

Included is this salute to the fallen:

> *Their strong arms crumble in the dust,*
> *And their bright swords have gathered rust;*
> *Their memory is our sacred trust,*
> *Michigan, my Michigan.*

The final stanza reflects the pathos of war:

> *A grateful country claims them now,*
> *Michigan, my Michigan,*
> *And deathless laurel binds each brow,*
> *Michigan, my Michigan;*
> *And history the tale will tell,*
> *Of how they fought and how they fell,*
> *For that dear land they loved so well,*
> *Michigan, my Michigan.*

One woman who sought to hold high such a deathless laurel for her soldier husband was Elizabeth Bacon. Known as "Libbie," the Monroe native married George Armstrong Custer in her hometown in the social event of 1864. Her war memoir was never written, but an actress who portrayed Libbie in twentieth century productions took diary entries, notes and manuscripts and stitched them into a unified, chronological whole.[72] Although Mrs. Custer's use of some terms betrays the racial prejudices of the era, her descriptions of the Boy General reveal a persona quite different from popular understanding: in place of the vainglorious and reckless image appears a much humbler individual born for warfare, yet considerate both of his men and captured former comrades at West Point. While one might chalk this imagery up to Libbie Custer's attempt at rehabilitating a tarnished reputation after Little Big Horn, the texts of letters and other contemporary materials are corroborating evidence.

At the same time, frequent references to "my husband" rather than something more formal keep reminding the reader of the fondness she felt for her soldier spouse. Mrs. Custer never remarried after the events of June 25, 1876, spending over a half-century after his death cherishing his memory, writing about their life together, seeking to enshrine the Boy General who had led the Michigan Cavalry Brigade into action during the war for the Union. She was no junior partner. An historian would adjudge that "no scholar ever has or ever will undertake a biography of George Armstrong Custer without due attention to his marriage and the character of his wife."[73]

One female contribution originated on July 20, 1861, the day before the Battle of First Bull Run, but concluded at war's end. A community meeting held in Detroit that July day resolved "to erect a monument to our 'heroic dead,'" but the lengthening magnitude of the conflict caused the project to be deferred. In July 1865, after collapse of the Confederacy, the monument effort resumed, with funds being sought from all elements of Michigan society. Chief among the supporters were "various auxiliary Ladies Monument Associations"[74] whose carefully husbanded funds helped make the imposing Soldiers and Sailors Monument in Campus Martius a reality soon after.

Women made many and varied contributions to Michigan's participation in the conflict. They served at home and at the front, doing their part for victory. Without their efforts, the state's response would have suffered. The Michigan women of the Civil War era helped secure the Union's triumph.

Chapter 6

WAR ON WATER

The waters outlining Michigan do more than shape the state and provide recreational outlets for its citizens; they have served as a moat, providing protection from hostile forces. Like all such water-based defenses, however, they require only appropriate countermeasures to make them ineffective. At several points, geography places Michigan in proximity to a foreign nation. In 1861 at Detroit, the guardian of the boundary was Fort Wayne, a muster point and drill ground for Michigan troops before they headed off to the battlefield. Far up at the Soo, Fort Brady served as the first line of defense. Military installations at Mackinac Island and other locations also resisted the potential of attack. Almost the entire Michigan–Canada border, though, lay miles from shore in the middle of Lakes Superior, Huron and Erie. Today, that line is the longest undefended border in the world. A century and a half ago, Canada's connection to Great Britain and its proximity to northern states like Michigan shaped a different strategic setting.

A single warship plied the waters of the Great Lakes in defense of the United States. The USS *Michigan* was a paddle steam frigate, but its significance eclipsed that status as the lone navy ship on the inland seas. Constructed in 1842 and launched the next year, it was the first iron-hulled steam warship in the U.S. fleet. Its mission was to guard four of the five Great Lakes, omitting only Lake Ontario because of the falls at its western end. The vessel's armament consisted of "pivoting shell guns mounted on its centerline,"[75] a revolutionary improvement in firepower. The *Michigan* could outrun any ship afloat, and, in case of battle

USS *Michigan.*

damage, its system of watertight compartments improved the likelihood of continued buoyancy. Forerunner to the famed USS *Monitor*, the iron vessel was designed to act independently of a fleet and either outgun or outrun its enemy.

The *Michigan* was a player in the "battle of Lake Erie," the most spectacular maritime incident on the Great Lakes during the Civil War. On September 19, 1864, the passenger steamer *Philo Parsons* departed Detroit bound for Sandusky, Ohio. Such an excursion was a forerunner of the trek millions of Michiganders would later take to that below-the-border destination to experience a different kind of wild ride. At a couple points along its route, the ship took on passengers who actually were Confederate plotters intent on using the ship for a daring exploit. Their plan: attack and capture the *Michigan*, free thousands of Confederates imprisoned at Johnson Island near Sandusky and convert the warship into a Great Lakes raider for the South. Not only would the Confederacy gain a significant manpower increase—among the captives were seven generals and the son of former vice president John C. Breckinridge—it would receive a huge morale boost. And the captured ship would wreak havoc on commercial traffic all through the lakes and St. Lawrence rivershed, mirroring destruction of Northern merchant ships on the oceans.

On land, a key player was a veteran of Nathan Bedford Forrest's cavalry. On water, the mastermind was a Scotsman with experience in irregular warfare.

Gaining control of the *Philo Parsons* by force (several crewmembers were injured) just past Put-in-Bay before its arrival at Kelley's Island, the Rebels redirected the vessel toward Sandusky Bay and the island prison camp just inside. The plan was abandoned, though, when most of the plotters grew fearful that the formidable *Michigan*, anchored in the harbor, had been warned. In truth, the plot had been uncovered. Turning about, the *Philo Parsons* headed back to the Canadian side of the Detroit River for an escape. Though most fled successfully, some Confederates were captured and imprisoned at Johnson's Island, an ironic outcome given their mission. When in range of the *Michigan*, the task of trying to take the warship proved too much. Its design had worked even without firing a shot.[76]

For Michigan's neighbors, the American Civil War would influence the shape of the Canadian confederation to come. While they may know something about the war, "[f]ew Canadians realize that, although it was primarily an American tragedy, it also stands as a defining event" in their history.[77] Tens of thousands of Canadians fought in the war[78]—some five thousand died—and twice during its course, Canada, as a constituent part of Great Britain, approached belligerency with the United States. History has treated the northern front as a sideshow, yet the Confederacy's failure to use Michigan's northern neighbor as a staging ground to open a second front contributed to the final outcome.

With its thousands of miles of fresh water coastline and a fast-moving river that flows by its largest city, Civil War Michigan could be expected to field a large contingent of sailors for the U.S. Navy. The identity of most is not known, but one mariner from Michigan deserved a better fate.

Detroiter William Gouin enlisted at Boston, Massachusetts, on January 1, 1862. He began his navy service on board the USS *Ohio* before transfer to the USS *Kearsarge*. The sloop-of-war was designed to hunt down Confederate raiders, and on June 19, 1864, it discovered the CSS *Alabama* in the harbor at Cherbourg, France. The exploits of the *Alabama* in attacking and sinking Union merchant ships was already legendary. Rather than holding in or making a run, the *Alabama* came out to face the Federal warship—and in an hour was ablaze and sinking. The superior firepower of the *Kearsarge* and its defensive armament gave it the advantage. Remarkably, the U.S. ship's crew suffered only three wounded in the battle and one killed. Seaman Gouin died on June 27, in the hospital at Cherbourg from wounds received during the engagement.

A surgeon aboard the ship recounted his impressions of Gouin:

> [Gouin's] *behavior during and after battle were worthy of the highest praise. Stationed at the after pivot-gun he was seriously wounded in the leg by the explosion of a shell; in agony, and exhausted from the loss of blood, he dragged himself to the forward hatch, concealing the severity of his injury, so that his comrades would not leave their stations for his assistance.*[79]

Though the only fatality, Gouin was not the only Michigander aboard. Fred Walden, also of Detroit, had enlisted for service as a coal heaver on the *Kearsarge* at Cadiz, Spain, on January 26, 1864, under the alias of John Pope. He also experienced the memorable sea battle and was discharged on November 30, 1864.[80]

American naval lore includes Commodore Dewey's famous order at the Battle of Manila Bay during the later Spanish-American War, "You may fire when ready, Gridley." The latter officer was captain of the *Olympia*, flagship of Dewey's squadron and a Civil War veteran. Charles V. Gridley had two Michigan connections. He was "attached" to the *Michigan* on the Great Lakes from 1870 to 1872. First, though, he had been appointed to the Naval Academy from Hillsdale, Michigan. An Indiana native whose family moved when he was quite young, he attended Hillsdale College until obtaining an appointment to Annapolis at age sixteen on September 26, 1860. Graduating in 1863, he served as an ensign aboard the USS *Oneida* from 1863 to 1865 as part of the West Gulf Blockading Squadron.[81] During the Battle of Mobile Bay in August 1864—occasion of another famous naval expression—his conduct received commendation as "beyond all praise."[82] Ironically, Gridley's final resting place is Erie, Pennsylvania, the port of station for the *Michigan*.

A complete accounting of the service of Michigan sailors is not found in postwar reporting. The record does reveal that 598 enlistments were credited to Michigan by the War Department. Of the 13 regular officers listed in the Michigan adjutant general's compendium, 2 served during the war in the U.S. Marine Corps, 1 commanded a ship in the assaults on Fort Fisher, 3 served aboard Admiral David Farragut's flagship USS *Hartford*, 1 served on the *Michigan* and 1 fought in Farragut's squadron at Vicksburg and Port Hudson. Several were wounded in action. "Of the services of Michigan men in the navy, during the war, there is unfortunately but little on record."[83] History may not have adequately written up their contributions to eventual victory, but that is history's fault.

Chapter 7

SPECIAL FORCES

On the southeast corner of the state capitol grounds in Lansing, more hidden than others, is a realistic statue of a Michigan soldier. The image is not just of any infantryman aiming a rifle. In October 1915, a half-century after the war and with the legislature's approval, the survivors of the First Michigan Sharpshooters came to town to dedicate their monument. Always a resourceful bunch, despite diminished numbers they had raised the necessary funds themselves.

From much of Michigan and from all walks of life they had been recruited for the Union army. Mustered in on July 7, 1863, the regiment saw action west of the Appalachians in defending against Morgan's Raid and then made its way east to fight at the Wilderness, Spotsylvania and Petersburg. The regiment was credited as one of the first two units to enter Petersburg in April 1865 after its forced abandonment by Lee's army. An inscription on the monument states that of a total enrollment of 981 soldiers, 113 were killed or died of wounds, 41 died as prisoners of war, 109 died of disease, 353 were discharged for wounds and disability and 365 remained to be mustered out on August 7, 1865.

Among that number were 145 Native Americans. From mostly the northern part of the Lower Peninsula, these men wore Union blue for a Michigan unit. Although they made up a small percentage of the total enrolled, each one had agreed to risk his life on the battlefield to preserve the United States of America. The adjutant general's report does not refer to them as Native Americans. That term was reserved for those who were not first-generation

The "Michigan Bridge" built by the First Engineers and Mechanics at Bridgeport, Alabama, in 1863.

immigrants. Rather, the report simply calls them Indians. Nonetheless, it does not appear to tally them in the "Total foreign" column but in the "Total Americans" figures. Despite nineteenth-century America's outlook, these Michiganders fought in the struggle for freedom and equality.[84]

During a later contest that touched on the same themes, actor John Wayne starred in a motion picture portraying *The Fighting Seabees*. These "construction battalions" performed their duties under hazardous conditions in the Pacific theater, arriving on the scene soon after the Marines to erect buildings, construct airfields and build bridges. They were trained to return enemy fire when necessary. Nearly a century earlier, the Seabees' forerunners were enlistees in the First Michigan Engineers and Mechanics. The regiment was comprised of artisans, craftsmen, railroad men and engineers, whose work advanced ultimate victory for the North by building and maintaining the infrastructure upon which the Union armies depended. And they fought Confederate units when attacked. Frequently separated by many miles due to the far-flung nature of their projects, the soldiers and their officers kept supply lines open, telegraph messages flowing and fortifications strengthened. Their bridge-building—a precursor to an iconic Michigan structure that would later link its two peninsulas—was a signature skill.[85]

In December 1862, a unique command was formed from three regiments of horse soldiers, all from the same state, united under one general officer. The Army of the Potomac veterans would become "the only cavalry brigade in the service made up entirely of regiments from a single state."[86] The Michigan Cavalry Brigade later was bolstered by the addition of a fourth from the Peninsula State, thus combining the First, Fifth, Sixth and Seventh Michigan horse regiments. Six months later, their special status was enhanced on the eve of Gettysburg. Promoted from captain to brigadier general, George A. Custer of Monroe, Michigan,[87] was given command. The move was intended to instill élan in the Army of the Potomac's cavalry command, which was often bested by Rebel cavalry.[88] It succeeded wildly. Of Custer's exploits there is no shortage of telling and, in the Civil War, most fell in the favorable column. Without those he commanded, of course, Custer would never have reached the apogee of his fame. They were "an elite unit," the best brigade in the cavalry arm.[89]

A case in point is the encounter between the Michigan troopers and Jeb Stuart's cavalry at Hunterstown, Pennsylvania, late in the day on July 2, 1863. The Union Third Cavalry division had been ordered to protect the Federal right flank near the town. Their advance scouts came into contact in the main street of Hunterstown with the rearguard of one of Stuart's brigades commanded by Wade Hampton. Falling back, the Confederates regrouped near a farmhouse on the road to Gettysburg. Custer had been directed to engage the gray cavalry, and he ordered a company of the Sixth Michigan to charge the enemy. Almost immediately, he drew his sword and shouted to the surprised troopers, "I'll lead you this time boys—Come on!"

Custer led the lone company southward past the Felty farm and directly into Hampton's defenders near the Gilbert house. The Confederates were posted on both sides of the road, and the fighting was furious. In hand-to-hand combat, Custer's horse fell, trapping the Boy General underneath. Rebels began to surround the dismounted and frantic officer. One approached Custer either to capture or kill the prize.

Twenty-three-year-old private Norvill Churchill of the First Michigan, one of the general's orderlies, came to the rescue. Riding up, he shot the enemy soldier and reached down for his commander. Custer grabbed Churchill's arm, pulled himself up and seated himself as best he could, hanging onto the saddle for dear life. Churchill turned his horse, and the three raced toward comrades and safety with the rest of Company A following close by. In the space of a few minutes, several Union soldiers had been killed or wounded, but the quick thinking of a young man from Almont[90] had saved the new general and preserved him for action the next day, at East Cavalry Field at Gettysburg, and on many other fields of fire before war's end.[91] Churchill's commanding officer, coincidentally, was also twenty-three.[92]

Custer and Stuart went at it again on the third day at Gettysburg. On the far left Confederate flank, Stuart brought his cavalry to harass and circle around behind the Union lines, sewing confusion in coordination with George Pickett's charge at the Federal center. Interdicting him was a detached unit of the Union cavalry—Custer's Michigan Brigade. The field east of Gettysburg saw numerous charges between the two forces, including several led by Custer himself. He rode to the head of one column and shouted, "Come on, you Wolverines!" Stuart was blocked and withdrew.[93]

Custer's charmed life while cutting a conspicuous figure[94] meant harrowing escapes on a number of occasions. Not so for Noah H. Ferry of the Fifth

Noah H. Ferry was born on Mackinac Island on August 30, 1831. He served in the Fifth Cavalry and was killed in action at East Cavalry Field, Gettysburg, on July 3, 1863.

Michigan Cavalry. Born on Mackinac Island in 1831, he grew up in Grand Haven and entered the service as captain of Company F in August 1862. Promoted to major in December 1862, he coolly led troops at East Cavalry Field. His men revered him. While rallying his men, a Confederate bullet killed him instantly. His immediate commanding officer, Russell Alger, would write: "His death cast a deep gloom upon the entire Brigade. He was a gallant soldier, an exemplary man, and his loss was a great blow." His father traveled to Gettysburg after the battle to retrieve the body of his brave son. He was buried in Lake Forest Cemetery in Grand Haven.[95]

The Michigan Cavalry Brigade would take fearfully high casualties during the Overland Campaign. In May 1864, its losses totaled 45 percent: of 1,700 men in the brigade, 98 would be killed in action, 330 wounded and 348 missing. At Trevilian Station in June, "[b]attling alone in dense, tangled underbrush, the Wolverines sustained 416 casualties, including 41 killed, the highest for the cavalry in the entire war."[96]

In the western theater, the horsemen of Michigan wrote their own history. Perhaps the winner of the longest Civil War book title competition would be *A Hundred Battles in the West: St. Louis to Atlanta, 1861–65. The Second Michigan Cavalry with the Armies of the Mississippi, Ohio, Kentucky and Cumberland, under Generals Halleck, Sherman, Pope, Rosecrans, Thomas and Others; with Mention of a Few of the Famous Regiments and Brigades of the West*.[97] The lengthy description aptly suggests how the Second Michigan Cavalry fought on many of the western battlegrounds. Rendezvousing at Grand Rapids in October 1861, the regiment fought at Island No. 10, in the campaign and siege of Corinth, at Perryville, at Chickamauga, at Knoxville, under Sherman into Georgia and under Thomas during the Nashville campaign.

The regiment should be renowned for another cause. One of its commanders was Philip A. Sheridan. The citizens of Port Huron presented a horse (one account indicates he was foaled near Grand Rapids) to Company K of the Second Cavalry, and the animal found its way into Sheridan's possession. The three-year-old mount was presented by the officers to Sheridan, then colonel of the regiment, in the spring of 1862 when the regiment was stationed at Rienzi, Mississippi, and that is how he got his name. Over seventeen hands in height, powerfully built, he was one of the strongest horses that Sheridan ever had. And Rienzi was cool under fire.

At Cedar Creek in the fall of 1864, Sheridan made a ride aboard Rienzi that became the stuff of legend. Hearing the sound of battle many miles away from Winchester, Sheridan spurred the horse and raced toward the conflict. He encountered groups of dispirited Federals retreating along the road; waving his hat and shouting for them to turn around and fight, Sheridan—and Rienzi—helped turn the tide and deliver a smashing defeat to the Confederate forces in the Shenandoah Valley:

> *The distance from Winchester to Cedar Creek, on the north bank of which the Army of the Shenandoah lay encamped, is a little less than nineteen miles. As we debouched into the fields...the general would wave his hat to the men and point to the front, never lessening his speed as he pressed forward. It was enough. One glance at the eager face and familiar black horse and they knew him and, starting to their feet, they swung their caps around their heads and broke into cheers as he passed beyond them; and then gathering up their belongings started after him for the front, shouting to their comrades farther out in the fields, "Sheridan! Sheridan!" waving their hats and pointing after him as he dashed onward...So rapid had been our gait that nearly all of the escort save the commanding officer and a few of his best mounted men had been distanced, for they were more heavily weighted and ordinary troop horses could not live at such a pace.*[98]

The "Gallant Charge" of the Sixth Cavalry near Falling Waters on July 14, 1863. The illustration is by Edwin Forbes, *Harper's Weekly*.

Personal exploits on horseback were not the exclusive province of generals. After participating in the Corinth campaign in late 1862, Ransom Myers was wounded in a conflict in Kentucky, suffered an arm amputation and returned to Michigan. He was not yet finished. With one arm, he reenlisted in the Tenth Michigan Cavalry to serve as a courier. Though he could no longer easily fire a weapon, his disability did not mean he lacked the will to serve at the front. He was discharged at war's end, becoming a minister of the gospel and serving in another army.

The Tenth Michigan Cavalry was in on the demise of John Hunt Morgan, the "Mosby of the West." Morgan met his fate "at the hands of Tennessee Unionists—the Thirteenth and Ninth Tennessee Cavalry regiments, aided by the Tenth Michigan." After the Confederate general's escape from the Ohio Penitentiary, he began operating in east Tennessee and planned an attack on a brigade of Tennessee and Michigan troops near Knoxville. On September 3, 1864, he moved his troops to Greenville, the home of Vice President Andrew Johnson. Morgan went to sleep in town and was awakened during the night to find the Union troops he had planned to attack surrounding the house. This time, however, his escape went awry, and he was fatally shot. "The forces engaged on the Union side" were the Thirteenth and Eighth Tennessee and "Tenth Michigan, Major Newell" of Ypsilanti commanding.[99]

The Michigan adjutant general's report tells the story:

The 10th Michigan Cavalry, then in command of Major Newell, encamped near Bulls' Gap, is ordered by General Gillam to attack the enemy's camp [along the Greenville road]. *Marching all night, he dismounts his men at daylight and charges into Morgan's first camp, driving the enemy in hot haste, leaving their breakfast half cooked, and their dead and wounded. Reaching the second camp, the enemy is found in better condition. General Gillam comes up with the 9th Tennessee Cavalry (Colonel Brownlow), orders that regiment to the charge with sabres, but a sharp fire from the enemy drove the regiment back. The 13th Tennessee Cavalry (Colonel Miller) comes up, the enemy driving the 9th advances rapidly, with a large cavalry force, at least 1,000 strong, filling the road from fence to fence. The 10th Michigan opens fire at about half pistol range with carbines, and soon the road is blocked with dead and wounded men and horses. The enemy, confused, hastily falls back, pursued to the woods, but is shelled out and pushes on to Greenville; is again charged on, becomes demoralized, breaks up, and flees. Morgan and staff are discovered under shelter of a house; a company of the 13th Tennessee is sent to capture him; he rushes for his horse, but is shot in the attempt by a sergeant of the company.*[100]

Michigan not only participated in putting down the Mosby of the West, it was front and center in the end of Jeb Stuart out East. The Battle of Yellow Tavern was fought north of Richmond on May 11, 1864. The cavalry action resulted from Sheridan's pursuit of Stuart, defending his capital, and whose aggressiveness led him to engage the Federals despite being greatly outnumbered. Sheridan went on the attack, and a little after four o'clock in the afternoon, in a driving rain, his troops charged the Confederate position, breaking it. Seeing the rift in his defenses, Stuart galloped to the fore and rallied his troops, driving off the Union troopers. One of those Union soldiers was Private John A. Huff of the Fifth Michigan, who had been a member of Berdan's famed sharpshooters. With a single shot, Huff inflicted a mortal wound to Stuart's side. "Stuart's death befell in front of Custer's Michigan brigade and it was a Michigan man who fired the fatal shot."[101]

Hiram Berdan—his name symbolized the corps of expert marksmen he recruited who could inspire fear with their ability to hit faraway targets. With enlistments in the elite unit originating from many states including Michigan, the regiment played "a conspicuous part" at Chancellorsville in surrounding and capturing hundreds of prisoners of the Twenty-third Georgia and helping hold the center of the Union line when the day seemed lost. Berdan had lived in Plymouth, Michigan, from age six and "passed every leisure hour in the woods with his rifle"—"his rural Michigan background was ever reflected in his lifelong interest in the sport of target shooting."[102] From this unit came the marksman who ended Jeb Stuart's life.

Not all of the general office cavalry casualties were on the Confederate side. Toward the end of the third day at Gettysburg, after Pickett's charge had been repulsed, an action occurred beyond Big Round Top on the far Federal left flank. This time, it was twenty-five-year-old Elon J. Farnsworth, born in Michigan, who went to his fate:

It is remarkable that the most deliberate and desperate cavalry charge made during the Civil War passed so nearly unnoticed that the attention of the country was first drawn to it by reports of the enemy. The charge was directly ordered by General Meade and immediately after it was made he sent a congratulatory dispatch, and yet when the report went up that Farnsworth was killed and the regiment that he led all but annihilated, this order was withheld from the Official Report. The friends of Farnsworth attacked Kilpatrick for having ordered a wanton waste of life and he remained silent. If the charge had been on any other part of the field, or at an earlier hour of the day, it would have commanded wide attention. As it was, it was witnessed only by the enemy and by the few men at the batteries.

After the repulse of Pickett, Meade's attention was drawn to an apparent movement of the enemy's troops towards the right. His left wing was peculiarly unprotected. Law's brigade was firmly lodged on the side of Round Top, and the valley to which Longstreet's eye turned so eagerly was open. An order reached Kilpatrick to hurl his cavalry on the rear of Law's brigade and create so strong a diversion that Lee's plan would be disclosed.

There was an oppressive stillness after the day's excitement. I rode to the front and found General Kilpatrick standing by his horse. He showed great impatience and eagerness for orders. The great opportunity, which was to have hurled his two brigades across the open fields upon the right and rear of Pickett's broken columns had been allowed to pass. As I turned away an orderly dashed by shouting: "We turned the charge, nine acres of prisoners." In a moment an aide came down and Kilpatrick sprang into his saddle and rode towards him. The verbal order I heard delivered was: "Hood's division is turning our left; play all your guns; charge in their rear; create a strong diversion."

In a moment, Farnsworth rode up. Kilpatrick impetuously repeated the order. Farnsworth, who was a tall man with military bearing, received the order in silence. It was repeated. Farnsworth spoke with emotion: "General, do you mean it? Shall I throw my handful of men over rough ground, through timber, against a brigade of infantry?"

We rode out in columns of fours with drawn sabres. After giving the order to me, General Farnsworth took his place at the head of the 3rd Battalion.

The 3rd Battalion under Major (William) Wells, a young officer who bore a charmed life and was destined to pass through many daring encounters...moved out in splendid form to the left of the 1st Battalion, and swept in a great circle to the right around the front of the hill and across our path, then guiding to the left across the valley and up the side of the hill at the base of Round Top. Upon this hill was a field enclosed with heavy stone walls. They charged along the wall and between it and the mountain directly in the rear of several Confederate regiments in position and between them and the 4th Alabama. It was a swift...charge over rocks, through timber, under close enfilading fire. The rush was the war of a hurricane. The direction towards Devil's Den. At the foot of the declivity the column turned left, rode close to a battery, receiving the fire of its support, and swept across the open field and upon the rear of the Texas skirmish line. Farnsworth's horse had fallen; a trooper sprang from the saddle, gave the General his horse and escaped on foot. Captain Cushman and a few others with Farnsworth turned back. The 1st Battalion was again in motion. The enemy's sharpshooters appeared in the rocks above us and opened fire. We rode obliquely up the hill in the direction of Wells, then wheeling to the left between the picket line and the wall. From this point, part of my men turned back with prisoners. The head of the column leapt the wall, into the open field. Farnsworth, seeing the horsemen, raised his sabre and charged as if with an army. At almost the same moment his followers and what remained of the 1st Battalion cut their way through the 15th Alabama, which was wheeling into position at a run and offered little resistance. We charged in the same direction but on opposite sides of the wall that parallels Round Top and within two hundred paces of each other.

General Farnsworth fell in the enemy's lines with his sabre raised, dead with five wounds, and received a tribute for gallantry from the enemy that his superiors refused. There was no encouragement of on

Merritt Lewis, Seventh Cavalry (Grand Rapids), lost his right leg at Gettysburg.

looking armies, no cheer, no bravado. There was consecration and each man felt as he tightened his sabre belt that he was summoned to a ride of death.[103]

In the years after the war, artist and painter James Kelly successfully persuaded veteran officers to sit for sketches, portraits and small talk. One participant was General Alexander Pennington, who spoke of Custer with the familiarity of one who had seen him up close. Pennington recounted how an officer regarded the flamboyant Boy General as a "popinjay," until seeing his courage in battle: "My God, I've had enough of him!" Pennington described Custer as being possessed of "a boyish chuckle. I never heard him laugh heartily," and how he would carry "a canteen of cold tea on his saddle." Finally, he told of how Custer's horse ran away down Pennsylvania Avenue during the grand review, thanks to its pedigree in racing, the rider "looking like a blaze of glory."[104]

Equally so, the Michigan horsemen, sharpshooters and engineers blazed their names and units into glory.

Chapter 8

TURNING THE TIDE

On the heels of the Army of the Potomac's disaster on the Rappahannock in December 1862, Confederate president Jefferson Davis felt confident in making a prediction:

> *Out of this victory is to come that dissatisfaction in the North West which will rive the power of that section; and thus we see in the future the dawn—first separation of the North West from the Eastern States, the discord among them which will paralyze the power of both,—then for us future peace and prosperity.*[105]

Davis's reference to the "North West" subsumed Michigan. Would it grow dissatisfied after so many disappointments and follow the South's example, withdrawing from support of the war during 1863?

In May, Lee again defeated the Army of the Potomac in the Battle of Chancellorsville. It was perhaps his most spectacular victory, and the hopes of the North for a change of outcome in the eastern theater were again dashed. On the heels of his victory, Lee launched his second invasion of the North in late June. En route to head off the Rebels, the Army of the Potomac got shocking news that a new commander would have to lead it into battle. The tides of war seemed all in Lee's favor.

The Union defenders caught up to Lee outside of a crossroads town in southern Pennsylvania. Outnumbered by brigades of Confederate infantry,

Buford's troopers held them off early in the morning along the Chambersburg pike northwest of the village. Arriving infantry were thrown into battle as soon as they neared the field. Among them was the Twenty-fourth Michigan, the most recent addition to the Iron Brigade comprised of western regiments.

The moment was critical:

> *At an early hour on the 1st day of July we marched in the direction of Gettysburg, distant six or seven miles. The report of artillery was soon heard in the direction of this place, which indicated that our cavalry had already engaged the enemy. Our pace was considerably quickened, and about 9 A.M. we came near the town of Gettysburg, and filed off to the left...and were moved forward into line of battle on the double-quick...The brigade was ordered to advance at once, no order being given or time allowed for loading our guns...The order to charge was now given, and the brigade dashed up and over the hill, and down into the ravine through which flows Willoughby's Run, where we captured a large number of prisoners...In this affair the 24th Michigan occupied the extreme left of the brigade...The brigade...marched into the woods known as McPherson's woods, and formed in line of battle...the position was ordered to be held, and must be held at all hazards. The enemy advanced in two lines of battle, their right extending beyond and overlapping our left...The 19th Indiana, on our left,...was forced back. The left of my regiment was now exposed to an enfilading and cross fire, and orders were given for this portion of the line to swing back so as to face the enemy now on the flank...We made a desperate resistance; but the enemy accumulating in our front, and our losses being very great, we were forced to fall back...By this time the ranks were so decimated that scarcely a fourth of the force taken into action could be rallied...We had inflicted severe loss on the enemy, but their numbers were so overpowering and our own losses had been so great that we were unable to maintain our position, and were forced back, step by step, contesting every foot of the ground to the barricade.*[106]

This account was written by the regiment's colonel, Henry Morrow of Detroit. He had been wounded in the action, captured and released after the

Abel G. Peck, Twenty-fourth Infantry (Nankin), enlisted at age forty-two on August 6, 1862, as a color bearer. He was killed in action at McPherson's Woods on the first day of Gettysburg.

battle. He wrote of the losses being severe, which was no exaggeration. The regiment went into battle with 496 officers and enlisted men. It suffered 363 casualties; color bearers Charles Ballou, August Ernest, William Kelly and Abel Peck were killed, along with 8 officers: Gilbert Dickey of Detroit, Newell Grace of Detroit, Reuben Humphreyville of Livonia, Malachi O'Donnell of Detroit, Winfield Safford of Plymouth, Lucius Shattuck of Plymouth, William Speed of Detroit and Walter Wallace of Brownstown. The next morning, only 99 men answered roll call.[107]

The Twenty-fourth had bought time—time for the rest of the army to come up and time for those who followed to take heights south of Gettysburg and hold them on this first day of July against further Rebel attacks. The First Michigan Infantry reached the battlefield after midnight, having ruined their shoe leather at a furious pace. Initially held in reserve the next morning, it was directed to the front line around four o'clock in the afternoon and posted in a wheat field on the left flank between an elevation known as Little Round Top and the center along Cemetery Ridge. It numbered 20 officers and 125 soldiers. Their arrival was just in time:

> *We had no sooner got our line fully established than the enemy drove in our skirmishers and appeared in force in the edge of a wood on our front, within two hundred yards of our line. We ordered our men to fix bayonets, and commenced firing on the enemy with a deadly effect, driving him back with great loss. He, however, soon returned, and was a second time driven back with great loss. Our men stood up bravely under the storm of bullets sent against them, loading and firing as coolly as though on drill...We maintained our line, repulsing and holding in check the enemy until 7:30 P.M., when we were ordered to fall back, which we did in good order.*[108]

First Lieutenant John Pulford, Company A, Fifth Infantry, rose to brevet brigadier general for meritorious service.

Similar contributions were made at this location and in a nearby peach orchard by the 3rd, 4th and 5th Infantry. Colonel Harrison Jefferds of Dexter defended the flag of the 4th in hand-to-hand fighting and paid for it with his life. The 5th was noted in the brigade after-action report: "The unflinching bravery of the 5th Michigan, which sustained a loss of more than one-half of its numbers without yielding a foot of ground, deserves to be especially mentioned."[109] Its colonel, John Pulford of Detroit, suffered two wounds in the fighting.[110]

Little Round Top commanded the Union line, which stretched out from its northern slope onto a ridge near the town cemetery. Confederate forces had noted the hill's strategic position and mounted a strong force to take it on this second day. A brigade composed of a regiment each from New York and Pennsylvania, the Twentieth Maine and the Sixteenth Michigan were rushed to the top. Arriving "in the nick of time" just before the Rebels, the brigade quickly piled stones together from which to begin firing at the gray soldiers climbing toward them. The Sixteenth faced into the teeth of an assault from a legendary Texas brigade and, when ammunition supplies failed, they used rocks against the enemy: "It was a deadly strife, with hand to hand encounters, clashing bayonets, clubbed muskets, and rough stones dug in desperation from the face of the rough hillside."[111] Desperation led to a charge down the hill that, against the odds, drove the Confederates off. The hill remained in Union hands for the rest of the battle.

On the afternoon of July 3, the Seventh Michigan Infantry was posted at the very center of the Union line near a low stone wall and a small wood of trees. The men had marched nearly seventy-five miles in three days and fought the day before in support of their comrades at the Wheatfield and the Peach Orchard. Its complement was down to 14 officers and 151 men out of the original 900. The men had stacked rails, stones and earth in front of their line for protection, using sticks and boards as implements in the absence of shovels. Posted on low-slung Cemetery Ridge, it had a front-row seat for what might develop during the afternoon.

Around 1:00 p.m., over one hundred Confederate artillery pieces opened up on the position held by the Seventh and its brigade in an obvious attempt to prepare the way for a major assault. Fortunately, the enemy gunners miscalculated a bit, and their shells landed primarily to the rear of the Union front-line position. At 3:00 p.m., the firing ceased, and thousands of Confederate infantry began to march out from under the protection of trees, form up in parade ground fashion and start off across the intervening farm fields to assault the Federal position. They came in several lines—waves, as it were. These were the troops who had been victors on the Peninsula, at the two Manassas battles, at Fredericksburg and Chancellorsville. Watching as they marched to the attack was its mastermind, Robert E. Lee, who had again and again correctly calculated how to impose defeat on his adversary.

Opposing the oncoming Rebel force was a line of blue infantry that included the Seventh. Federal artillery commander Henry Hunt sought to aid their defense and now brought a hundred Union guns to bear on the Rebel charge. Hunt seemed to be everywhere this fateful day. At midmorning, he had carefully inspected the entire line in the center to verify that all the Federal batteries were in good condition and fully supplied. His instructions to the batteries and chiefs of artillery were to fire their guns deliberately and concentrate it on one enemy battery at a time—not stopping until each was silenced. Hunt was on the summit of Little Round Top at 1:00 p.m., when the Confederate guns opened up at the center. He had immediately left for the Artillery Reserve park to order all replacement batteries prepared to move up at a moment's notice. Next he had proceeded along the line, under fire, to replace batteries that were disabled by the Confederate barrage. About 2:30 p.m., he ordered his gunners to gradually cease their return fire to conserve ammunition for the infantry charge he expected to come and, in the process, perhaps deluded the Confederates that the cannonade had silenced enough Union guns to justify advancing their infantry. At 3:00 p.m., as the enemy infantry advanced, he ordered new batteries into position to replace exhausted ones and positioned guns to operate both in front and in flank of the oncoming wave. As he waited for their arrival near the stone wall, Hunt sat on his horse and drew his sidearm, ready to help repel the thousands of soldiers who were approaching the Federal line.

The brigade commander of the Seventh was Norman Hall, and here is what he would write afterward of the next several moments:

> *My line was single, the only support...having been called away... There was a disposition in the men to reserve their fire for close quarters, but when I observed the movement the enemy was endeavoring to execute, I caused the Seventh Michigan and Twentieth Massachusetts Volunteers to open fire at about 200 yards.*

The deadly aim of the former regiment was attested by the line of slain within its range. This had a great effect upon the result, for it caused the enemy to move rapidly at one point and consequently to crowd in front—being occasioned at the point where his column was forming, he did not recover from this disorder.

There was but a moment of doubtful contest in front of the position of this brigade. The enemy halted to deliver his fire, wavered, and fled, while the line of the fallen perfectly marked the limit of his advance. The troops were pouring into the ranks of the fleeing enemy that rapid and accurate fire, the delivery of which victorious lines always so much enjoy, when I saw that a portion of the line...on my right had given way, and many men were making to the rear as fast as possible, while the enemy was pouring over the rails that had been a slight cover for the troops.

Having gained this apparent advantage, the enemy seemed to turn again and re-engage my whole line...I was forced to order my own brigade back from the line, and move it by the flank under a heavy fire. The enemy was rapidly gaining a foothold; organization was mostly lost; in the confusion commands were useless, while a disposition on the part of the men to fall back apace or two each time to load, gave the line a retiring direction. With the officers of my staff and a few others, who seemed to comprehend what was required, the head of the line, still slowly moving by the flank, was crowded closer to the enemy and the men obliged to load in their places. I did not see any man of my command who appeared disposed to run away.

The line remained in this way for about ten minutes, rather giving way than advancing, when, by a simultaneous effort upon the part of all the officers I could instruct, aided by the general advance of many of the colors, the line closed with the enemy, and, after a few minutes of desperate, often hand-to-hand fighting, the crowd—for such had become that part of the enemy's column that had passed the fence—threw down their arms and were taken prisoners of war, while the remainder broke and fled in great disorder...Generals Garnett and Armistead were picked up near this point, together with many colonels and officers of other grades.

Twenty battle-flags were captured in a space of 100 yards square...Between 1,500 and 2,000 prisoners were captured at the point of attack...Piles of dead and thousands of wounded upon both sides attested the desperation of assailants and defenders.[112]

Among the dead was the Seventh's lieutenant colonel, Amos Steele of Mason, killed while leading his men to defeat the assault.[113]

The battle—and perhaps the war—had hung in the balance. Michigander Hall, veteran of so many actions, evaluated what had happened:

In claiming for my brigade and a few other troops the turning point of the battle of July 3, I do not forget how liable inferior commanders are to regard only what takes place in their own front, or how extended a view it must require to judge of the relative importance of different points of the line of battle. The decision of the rebel commander was upon that point; the concentration of artillery fire was upon that point; the din of battle developed in a column of attack upon that point; the greatest effort and greatest carnage was at that point; and the victory was at that point.[114]

"At that point." Here it was that a "rain of missiles," a "terror-spreading" barrage, had been concentrated on their position. Here it was that the gray infantry marched forward with "an appearance of being fearfully irresistible."[115] Here it was that near the stone wall, behind a rail fence, the Seventh Michigan stood against the irresistible at the very moment when the battle would turn. Ever after, this point would be known, and commemorated by monument and memory, as the "High Water Mark of the Confederacy."

Michigan cavalry also played a part in the victory on the third day. On the far right of the Union positions, the cavalry brigade under the command of General George Custer met the mounted legions of Wade Hampton, right-hand to Jeb Stuart. The Boy General and his Michigan riders "charged in close column upon Hampton's brigade, using the saber only, and driving the enemy from the field."[116] On the left, the other cavalry boy general from Michigan, Elon Farnsworth of Green Oak Township, made a desperate charge that cost him his life.[117]

July was also an important month in the other theater of war. The day after the battle at Gettysburg concluded, Grant's campaign to take the Confederate stronghold at Vicksburg, Mississippi, concluded with the surrender of the town and thirty thousand defenders. For weeks the Union army had marched through Mississippi, defeating each Rebel contingent it confronted, until finally trapping the Confederates and laying siege to the river town. Michigan troops were in the campaign and helped capture Vicksburg, closing off the Mississippi River to Confederate navigation for the remainder of the war. The Second, Sixth, Eighth, Twelfth, Fifteenth, Twentieth and Twenty-seventh Infantry Regiments had marched, fought and assaulted the Rebels until achieving victory in the surrender on the Fourth of July.

While eyes back home were glued to the reports emerging from Gettysburg and Vicksburg, the Twenty-fifth Michigan Infantry was trying to save Louisville, Kentucky. Recruited from towns like Buchanan, Galesburg, Holland, Niles and Three Rivers, five companies were defending a bridge across the Green River at Tebbs Bend on the morning of July 4. Confederate cavalry commanded by General John H. Morgan outnumbered them four to one. He ordered the regiment to surrender—the cause of the 260 Michigan

Lorin L. Comstock (Adrian), served in the First Infantry (three months) and as a lieutenant colonel of the Seventeenth Infantry. He died on November 25, 1863, after being hit with a musket ball by a Rebel sharpshooter at Knoxville.

troops was hopeless. Colonel Orlando Moore of Schoolcraft replied, "This being the Fourth of July, I cannot entertain the proposition of surrender." Morgan made eight attacks on their entrenchments. At the medical station, treating the wounded, a surgeon discovered something unusual about his patient: she was Lizzie Compton, a woman disguised as a man in order to fight for her country. Her services under fire helped turn Morgan away and produce an unlikely victory.

In the fall, the Federal force at Knoxville found itself under siege. Among their number was Charles Howard Gardner, a Michigan boy serving as drummer in his unit. Gardner had grown up in Flint; when Charley was thirteen, his

Charles H. Gardner, musician, Eighth Infantry (Flint), enlisted for three years at age fourteen. He died December 21, 1863, at Knoxville from wounds received on December 1.

father joined the Second Michigan Infantry, and his favorite teacher, S.C. Guild, signed up with the Eighth. Charley enlisted with his teacher's unit as part of its band. He was, after all, too young to fight. The outcome of their volunteering would be the same. Charley's father died while in service of typhoid fever; Guild was killed in action. The young Gardner decided not to quit and remained with his regiment during the siege in Knoxville. During action he was shot, but the wound did not initially appear fatal. After the siege was lifted and the Eighth had fought off the Rebels, the wounded Charley Gardner was sent back to Detroit for recuperation. He never made it. His mother and siblings, anxiously awaiting a happy return after losing the other two, would have to learn of Gardner's death en route.

After Grant's great victory at Vicksburg, he was assigned to replace Rosecrans at Chattanooga when the latter let himself get entrapped at that Tennessee River town. The first step Grant took was to open up a solid supply line, for the Union troops were on short rations. Michigan engineers built a magnificent bridge over the river as a key part of eliminating the shortage. Hemming in the besieged Union army, the Rebels sat atop a naturally strong position of Lookout Mountain on the west and Missionary Ridge to the south. The Rebel commander, Braxton Bragg, thought his position was impregnable.[118] On Saturday, November 25, his troops fully supplied, Grant launched attacks on both wings of the Confederate position. After the passage of several hours, neither was succeeding, so in late afternoon, he directed an assault on the center, hoping to draw defenders away from their flanks and make those attacks victorious. What happened next surprised even the unflappable Grant.[119]

The Eleventh Michigan, under the command of William Stoughton of Sturgis,[120] was posted in the Union center, to the left of troops commanded by Philip Sheridan. They faced an open field of nearly a half-mile's length in front of Missionary Ridge. Rebel rifle pits were located halfway up the slope, and a strong breastwork with cannons in place here and there was visible at the top. Bragg's confidence did seem well placed. Receiving Grant's order to attack, the regiment and the whole line in the center moved forward toward this "impregnable mountain wall that blotted out half the sky."[121] The advance was immediately shelled by Confederate artillery, but they continued to move steadily toward the base of the hill and a line of pickets. The thin gray line was sent fleeing up the hill, but this was little achievement. The Rebel fire upon their position at the base was growing ever more destructive, so Stoughton ordered a charge up the slope upon the first line of rifle pits. Scrambling up the side of the ridge, the Union infantry took the position and regrouped during a brief respite. They soon discovered it was no place to stay—the "rising slope was an obvious deathtrap...From the crest of the ridge the Confederates were sending down a sharp plunging fire."[122]

Another order was given: "At the command the whole line sprung forward in gallant style and moved rapidly up the steep and difficult ascent. When near the crest they dashed forward with a shout of victory, routing the enemy and driving him from his stronghold, and capturing a large number of prisoners and one piece of artillery."[123]

The Eleventh had done what seemed impossible. Marching across an open plain in full sight of the enemy, undergoing artillery fire all the while, taking the picket line at the base, then the rifle pits halfway up and then assaulting

Albert Sonewald, First Infantry (Ann Arbor), was a veteran of battles from Mechanicsville to Gettysburg. He died of disease in a Washington, D.C. hospital on October 31, 1863.

the breastworks on the summit, they had gone into battle with 255 officers and men, suffered 34 casualties and won for their command—and Grant, who would soon be sent East—a great victory.

As the year was ending, the voters of Troy Township went to the polls on December 28 to decide whether to approve a new tax. Proceeds would be used to encourage enlistments by paying $100 to each man who volunteered to join the Union military. The bounty was one of many proposed to Michigan voters in local and state elections to encourage enlistment. In the midst of the war, the people of this community had to confront imposing higher taxes on themselves in order to send more soldiers off on behalf of the Union. Troy voters said "yes."

Jefferson Davis had proven a poor prophet. How would the record be written of Michigan's participation during 1863?

> *They bore a conspicuous and gallant part in the ever memorable campaigns under General Hooker in Virginia, and General Meade in Pennsylvania, at the defense of Knoxville by General Burnside, at the capture of Vicksburg by General Grant, and on the celebrated Kilpatrick raid against Richmond. They were also engaged in the campaign of General Rosecrans against Chattanooga.*[124]

Employing neutral terms like "conspicuous" and "memorable" suggested mixed results; "gallant" left nothing to judgment. In truth, this summary far understated the sacrifices and valor contributed during this year by Michigan's infantry, cavalry, artillery soldiers and citizens back home.

Chapter 9

THE FIGHTING 102ND

In June 1967, urban violence erupted in Michigan's largest city after a police raid on a blind pig backfired. It was a hot summer, the war in Vietnam was raging and racial tensions between the African American community and the police department boiled over. In June 1943, a civil disturbance erupted in Detroit when violence broke out between racial groups. Social and migration changes caused by World War II set teeth on edge. Both riots had a Civil War antecedent, reflecting unfinished business about race.

On March 6, 1863, after the trial of a "colored" man resulted in conviction for assaulting a white female, rioters—dissatisfied with the resulting jail sentence—took to Detroit streets to inflict injury on persons and property. No draft riot like the infamous New York City event of July 1863, it was, by all accounts, racially driven.[125] The media contributed to the discord: the *Detroit Advertiser & Tribune* blamed the event on racially oriented coverage by its competitor, the *Detroit Free Press*; for its part, the *Free Press* blamed the event on those who were disrupting the existing social order.[126] At the same time whites in Detroit were inflicting death and destruction on blacks, in Lansing, the governor of Michigan was calling for more racial equality and equal rights. A civil war seemed to be raging within the state over the issue of freedom: for whom and under what conditions?

About 45,000 people lived in Detroit according to the 1860 census. Some 6,799 blacks were recorded in Michigan that year, with a quarter of their population residing in Detroit. On April 25, 1861, reacting to Fort Sumter

Felix C. Balderry, Eleventh Infantry (Leonidas Township), enlisted at age twenty-one on December 7, 1863, for three years. A "South Sea Islands immigrant," he was most likely Filipino.

and mobilization of troops to answer Lincoln's call, black Detroiters met at the Second Baptist Church to declare:

> 1. That we love this land of our nativity, above all lands.
> 2. That when the government of the State of Michigan manifests a deposition to recognize us as men and citizens,…then we will sacrifice our lives, if necessary, in defense of the flag of our country.
> 3. That…as men whose hearts are with the union and the flag, we beg the government of Michigan to place us in such a position that we may be able to prove the courage, devotion and patriotism of our people.

4. Nevertheless, that if the State of Michigan is ever invaded we hold ourselves ready and willing, in common with other men to repel such invasion at all hazards and to the last extremity.[127]

African Americans elsewhere in Michigan made similar offers.[128]

Such volunteerism could not be accepted under Federal law. The second Militia Act of 1792 made eligible for service "each and every free able-bodied white male citizen" of a state. Lincoln's call for three-months' soldiers, invoking this statutory authority, could not lawfully enable nonwhites to fight the Southern rebellion. The lengthening course of the war, however, made necessary a reappraisal of this policy.

In Michigan, the campaign to advocate reversal of this policy began early. Governor Blair supported black enlistment and emancipation. The *Detroit Advertiser & Tribune* called for the enlistment of blacks, given their obvious "ability to serve in a [*sic*] intelligent and courageous manner."[129] People of color in Detroit were "especially vocal"[130] in support of such a step. Michigan's two U.S. senators, Zachariah Chandler and Jacob Howard, were on the side of such efforts in Congress. A revised militia act, passed with their support in July 1862, permitted enlistment "for the purpose of constructing intrenchments [*sic*], or performing camp service or any other labor, or any military or naval service for which they may be found competent, persons of African descent."

Such service merited reward:

Any man or boy of African descent, who by the laws of any State shall owe service or labor to any person who, during the present rebellion, has levied war or has borne arms against the United States, or adhered to their enemies by giving them aid and comfort, shall render any such service as is provided for in this act, he, his mother and his wife and children, shall forever thereafter be free, any law, usage, or custom whatsoever to the contrary notwithstanding.

When the vote for the bill came up in the summer of 1862, both senators were steadfast in seeking the maximum opportunity for blacks to serve in the military.[131]

In the spring of 1863, not content to limit duties to support roles, Governor Blair and Senator Chandler jointly applied to the War Department for

Kinchen Artis, Company H, First Colored Infantry, enlisted at age thirty-seven on December 19, 1863, at Battle Creek for three years.

authority to raise a regiment of colored infantry. *Advertiser & Tribune* editor Henry Barnes separately wrote for permission. They would have to wait until July for the War Department to issue approval—but once received, little more delay occurred. Within just a couple of weeks, Adjutant General Robertson authorized Barnes to begin enrollment in the first Michigan regiment of persons of color. The choice of a newspaperman to lead the effort, and his commissioning as colonel of the regiment, meant that someone with no military experience would initially lead the Michigan contingent.

Six months later, on February 17, 1864, the First Michigan Colored Regiment mustered, 895 strong, and marched down Woodward Avenue to the approbation of onlookers. It had taken a while to achieve the requisite strength—not because of a lack of fortitude by Michigan blacks, but because their ranks had been reduced by bounties (army pay was lower than that of whites) and recruiting efforts from other northern states that lacked a significant African American population. To prevent the undermining of Michigan's contribution, the legislature acted to prohibit recruiting of Michigan men by out-of-state interlopers. In December 1863, the regimental leadership and band made a tour of the southern Michigan counties, stopping in Ypsilanti, Ann Arbor, Jackson, Niles, Cassopolis, Marshall and Kalamazoo. Traveling the circuit paid off, doubling the number of enlistments in just a few weeks.

After their mustering in, the regiment trained at Camp Ward just east of downtown Detroit.[132] In March, they embarked for Annapolis and further training. After arrival, Barnes resigned as colonel and returned to Detroit, with his mission to deploy black soldiers in the field accomplished. Detroiter Henry L. Chipman, a regular army captain at war's inception and an officer of high regard, was promoted from lieutenant colonel. The unit was transported to Hilton Head Island, South Carolina, in April and, on May 23, 1864, was redesignated as the 102nd United States Colored Troops (USCT) in accordance with War Department requirements.

As was typical with USCTs, the Michigan unit initially was assigned guard duty, rather than front-line service, of fortifications on the island and in Beaufort. In early August, they moved to Jacksonville, Florida, and first "saw the elephant." On August 11, a march inland to the village of Baldwin was met by a troop of Confederate cavalry seeking to protect the rail junction. The rebels attacked—and were repulsed by the 102nd. This first successful encounter was followed up by a five-day, one-hundred-mile march farther into Florida, tearing up track and destroying rolling stock. Their route passed the battleground at Olustee where, just months earlier, a Union force had been defeated. If accounts of that conflict were accurate, casualties in the black troops involved had included post-battle hostilities.

At the end of August, the regiment was transferred back to Beaufort. On November 28, it was part of an expeditionary force that steamed up the Broad River to sever the Charleston & Savannah Railroad near Pocotaligo, South Carolina, and support Sherman's campaign against Savannah. Disembarking at Boyd's Landing, it marched inland and, on November 30, encountered an entrenched Confederate force at Honey Hill. During the battle, a section of the 3rd New York Artillery was cut down by Southern fire, jeopardizing its ordnance. The 102nd was ordered to secure and bring off the cannons. After an initial attempt did not succeed, an officer and thirty men thrice rushed forward to secure the guns where Rebel artillery and sharpshooters had killed off the gunners. Each rush retrieved an artillery piece. Their commander was later awarded the Medal of Honor and, in his after-action report, Colonel Chipman wrote: "Too high praise cannot be awarded to Lieutenant [Orson] Bennett[133] for the gallant manner in which he led his men in that perilous enterprise, nor to his men who so faithfully followed their leader." With one-fifth of the force suffering casualties—sixty-six in total—the heroism of these men could not be argued.[134]

In January, the regiment again began a campaign to support Sherman's march northward. The men made several expeditions into the countryside, attacking and dispelling Confederate cavalry and destroying railroads. On February 27, they entered the captured city of Charleston, having "ransacked every plantation on our way and burnt up every thing we could not carry away."[135] An early March expedition found them moving toward Georgetown, then turning toward the heartland, to begin destruction of rail lines and equipment through Sumter(ville) and Camden. After taking the latter town, the force marched south toward Stateburg until, on April 18, meeting Confederates where Swift Creek ran into the Wateree River at Boykin's Mill. The Rebel force was across the creek and on higher ground, with marshes protecting the approaches. Several unsuccessful assaults were made until the 102nd was ordered to flank the Confederates on their right; with "the aid of a negro guide they succeeded in crossing on a log." Having a lodgment to turn the Rebel line, the entire force then charged their position and succeeded when "the enemy gave way." The next day saw the same kind of encounter at Rafting Creek, and the same flanking tactic was employed to the same level of success. Driving the Rebs off, the force resumed its march back toward Georgetown and further warfare.

It was no longer necessary. On April 21, during a midday rest stop at Fultons Post Office south of Manchester, a detachment of Confederates appeared, bearing a flag of truce. The Southerners conveyed the imminent surrender of Joseph Johnston to Sherman. With Lee having capitulated in Virginia, no other major Confederate force was in the field east of the Mississippi—thus, the war was effectively over. The expedition had been a success, with minimal losses. Chipman was recognized for "excellent service" thanks to the performance of his troops.[136] The regiment spent the next five months in Charleston on occupation duty.

Flag of the First Colored Infantry.

On September 30, 1865, the 102nd USCT ceased to exist when the veterans were mustered out of Federal service. They returned to Detroit, arriving on October 17 and 19. A total of 1,555 had enlisted and, according to U.S. provost marshal records, 1,387 men served in the unit. Approximately 150 deserted, a typical attrition rate during the war, with a desertion rate of only 1.2 percent in the field. About 10 percent never came home: 6 were killed in action, 5 died of wounds and 129 died of disease. Their average age was 25.8; some were younger than 18. Approximately 43 percent were farmers, because a full two-thirds had come from southwest Michigan, while 9 percent were from Detroit. Very few had been born in Michigan, for obvious reasons, but they did the state proud. Even the *Free Press* conceded that they had fought nobly.

Inspired by their service, fellow Michigander Sojourner Truth is credited with authoring lyrics of "The Valiant Soldiers," sung to the tune of "John Brown's Body."[137] Modern-era Detroiter Dudley Randall wrote this springtime poem in the honor of the soldiers of the 102nd:

Memorial Wreath
In the green month when resurrected flowers
Like laughing children ignorant of death,

Brighten the couch of those who wake no more,
Love and remembrance blossom in our hearts,
For you who bore the extreme sharp pang for us,
And bought our freedom with your lives.
 And now,
Honoring your memory, with love we bring
These fiery roses, white-hot cotton flowers
And violets bluer than cool northern skies
You dreamed of stooped in burning prison fields
When liberty was only a faint north star,
Not a bright flower planted by your hands
Reaching up hardy nourished with your blood.
Fit gravefellows you are for Douglass, Brown,
Turner and Truth and Tubman...whose rapt eyes
Fashioned a new world in this wilderness.
American earth is richer for your bones;
Our hearts prouder for the blood we inherit.

Chapter 10

THE GENERALS

S on of the Morning Star, Yellow Hair, Boy General: most Americans recognize one of Michigan's most famous military officers by such terms, for they refer to George Armstrong Custer of Little Big Horn fame. More than a decade before that encounter, Custer led the Michigan Cavalry Brigade to glory after his promotion from captain to brigadier general[138] on June 28, 1863, immediately before the Battle of Gettysburg. He was but one of three elevated that day. Wesley Merritt of New York was also promoted to brigadier general from captain; he went on to division command under Phil Sheridan. Custer and Merritt remain well known, the former for the fateful day in the Black Hills of South Dakota, the latter for, among other things, presiding over the inquiry into that event. What of the third appointee?

Elon John Farnsworth was born on July 30, 1837, in Green Oak Township, Michigan. He entered the University of Michigan in 1855 but left in 1858 to join the First Dragoons in the Mormon conflict in Utah. After the Civil War began, he led a cavalry regiment in a number of eastern theater engagements. On the road to Gettysburg, the cavalry commander of the Army of the Potomac recommended his promotion to brigadier general and command of the First Cavalry Brigade, Third Division. He led his troopers into action at Hanover Station on June 30, driving off Jeb Stuart's horsemen. At an action on July 1 en route to Gettysburg, Farnsworth was slightly wounded but remained in the saddle. The next day, after dark, brought on another skirmish at Hunterstown; then came the third day of the battle.

George A. Custer,
before fame.

Pickett's Charge at the center of the Union line had just failed, and the Army of Northern Virginia drew itself up to defend against a counterattack. Union commander Meade decided not to risk wide-scale offensive action. On the Federal left, however, Farnsworth was ordered by his immediate superior, General Judson Kilpatrick (nicknamed "Kill Cavalry"), to attack the Confederates' far right flank in coordination with Merritt's force.

Although Farnsworth protested that it was suicide, Kilpatrick insisted that he should charge with half of his brigade against the center of Law's slender line. Law by juggling his men about had neutralized Merritt's threat and had shifted what little weight he could spare against Farnsworth, who soon found himself running through a gauntlet of Confederate infantry no matter which way he

*turned. He put on a brilliant display of courage and horsemanship,
but the attack ended in a fiasco, including the death of Farnsworth.*[139]

The "gallant Farnsworth fell, heroically leading a charge of his brigade, against
the rebel infantry," suffering "five mortal wounds."[140] The site where he went
down, known today as South Cavalry Field, is a section of America's most
famous battlefield that is least visited. Farnsworth was twenty-five years old
and had been a general officer for six days.

Another Michigan-bred general fought with distinction at Gettysburg.
Henry J. Hunt was born to a military family at Detroit Barracks on September
14, 1819,[141] and spent part of his adolescence in Maumee, just across the Ohio
border. His appointment to West Point ended with a ranking in the middle
of the class (nineteenth of thirty-one).[142] Serving in the Mexican War and
the Mormon expedition, Hunt possessed extensive combat and leadership
experience when the Civil War began. His battery covered the retreat at First
Bull Run, and he was the tactical genius behind the massed batteries of Federal
artillery that decimated Rebel attacks at Malvern Hill, saving the Army of the
Potomac. Such contributions were echoed at Antietam and Fredericksburg;
notwithstanding, under General Joseph Hooker, his command was reduced
to a nominal level at the Battle of Chancellorsville, which Hunt argued, and
Hooker admitted, was an important factor in the Union defeat.

Arriving on the field at Gettysburg late on July 1, he was called upon the
next day to place batteries and ensure sufficient ammunition in all three sectors
of the defenses manned by the Army of the Potomac. His acumen helped stem
the looming disaster at the Peach Orchard and Wheatfield on the Union left.
It was on the third day, though, that he reached the pinnacle of his career.[143]

Hunt first had to ensure proper support for the Federal right flank at Culp's
Hill during the morning. Army commander Meade looked for Lee to attack in
the center, along Cemetery Ridge, and Hunt next busied himself in readying the
Union artillery for an infantry assault. While the Army of Northern Virginia
unleashed its entire artillery to soften up the Federal position for the charge,
Hunt kept admonishing his gunners to save and target their return fire. Such
carefulness resulted in a dispute with infantry general Winfield Hancock, who
wanted the return fire of cannons to embolden his soldiers as they awaited Lee's
assault. Hunt disagreed; the guns were best employed in hitting real artillery
targets and defending against massed infantry, not merely as morale boosters.

This hard-won wisdom paid off for the Union side once the Confederate batteries grew silent and long lines of infantry emerged from behind their positions. Stepping off for the mile-long hike across open fields to the Federal lines, the thousands of Rebels were an imposing sight—except to Henry Hunt. His artillerymen let loose with a storm of shot and shell that staggered the gray divisions and pushed them toward the left, squeezing the attack into a narrow section of the Union lines near a stone wall and copse of trees. To here, in the epicenter of danger, Hunt spurred his horse. He was the only mounted officer on Cemetery Ridge, conspicuous by his height, uniform and by firing a sidearm at the enemy.

Bruce Catton painted the scene in *Glory Road* when soldiers

> *heard the uproar of battle different from any they had ever heard before—"strange and terrible, a sound that came from thousands of human throats, yet was not a commingling of shouts and yells but rather like a vast mournful roar." There was no cheering, but thousands of men were growling and cursing without realizing it as they fought to the utmost limit of primal savagery...Gibbon was down with a bullet through his shoulder, Webb had been wounded, and Hancock was knocked off his horse by a bullet...Except for one valiant staff officer, there was not a mounted man to be seen. Hunt was in the middle of the infantry, firing his revolver.*[144]

General Alexander Webb, commander of the center of the Union line, would much later recount the scene to an illustrator:

> *I was dismounted. In fact, we were all dismounted...Could you typify the artillery, which were firing grapeshot over our heads into those fellows, by representing Hunt, the Chief of Artillery, on horseback, just looking over the rear of my lines. That's good!...Another thing I remember, I looked around and there I saw Hunt who had ridden up, and was popping at them with a revolver. I had to laugh; he looked so funny, up there on his horse, popping at them...He was right at the line, my men, you could put him here; that would introduce it...That's it. That is true. That is on oath, and the first time I have seen it correct...Kelly: Here is Hunt. Webb: Yes, make him coming*

up with some men. Kelly: Why did you laugh, when you said he used his pistol? Webb: Because he looked so funny picking at them; I did not need his little pistol.[145]

Hunt's horse was shot and went down, momentarily trapping the general's leg. Several of his gunners helped him up as Union infantry came running to push back the Southerners. In a moment, it was over. The Army of the Potomac, infantry and artillery together, had been too much for Pickett's charge. Henry Hunt had been instrumental in turning back the high tide of the Confederacy.[146] He went on to serve, but it would be hard to reach this pinnacle again.[147]

General Israel B. Richardson.

Not every general was so fortunate. At Antietam, Israel Richardson went down from an artillery shell wound while leading his division at Bloody Lane. Richardson was a five-year cadet at West Point, graduating toward the bottom (thirty-eighth in a class of fifty-two). His academic performance was eclipsed during the Mexican War, when he twice was brevetted for bravery. Resigning from the army in 1855, he moved to Pontiac, Michigan, to begin civilian life as a farmer.

The outbreak of war brought him back as captain of the Second Infantry. He commanded a brigade at First Bull Run and was promoted first to brigadier then major general. He fought during the Peninsula Campaign and at South Mountain. On September 17, 1862, he led his troops into the single bloodiest day of the war. After being wounded, he was taken to the Pry House, headquarters of army commander McClellan, behind the lines.[148] He had the honor of a visit from the president, and his wife came to his side to help his recuperation. Although not immediately life-threatening, Richardson's wound became infected, and he came down with pneumonia. On November 3, 1862, he died.

The site of his wounding is marked today on the Antietam battlefield just below the observation tower at the Sunken Road. Vehicles travel down Richardson Avenue to gain access to one of the most historic portions of any Civil War site. The marker, central on the battleground, is testimony to valor on that awful day:

> *I looked over my right shoulder and saw that gallant old fellow advancing on the right of our line, almost alone, afoot with his bare sword in his hand, and his face was as black as a thunder cloud; and well it might be, for some of our own men, turning their heads toward him, cried out, "Behind the haystack!" and he roared out, "God d—— the field officers!" I shall never cease to admire that magnificent fighting general who advanced with his front line, with his sword bare and ready for use, and his swarthy face, burning eye, and square jaw, though long since lifeless dust, are dear to me.*[149]

Like Richardson, Alpheus Williams had embraced Michigan later in life. Moving to Detroit in 1836 at the age of twenty-six, he made it his lifelong home—with one major interlude: military service for his state that began

General Alpheus S. Williams.

(unofficially) in 1860 before the war erupted and lasted until its end. He had no West Point background to commend himself to the Union effort, only service as a militia officer whose troops never got into action during the Mexican War. Commissioned a brigadier general in August 1861, he commanded troops in both theaters and assumed temporary command of the Twelfth Corps at Gettysburg on the right flank at Culp's Hill. "Pap" Williams, as his troops affectionately called him, never rose beyond brigade rank, yet he was one of the most reliable officers of the War. Sherman wrote of him: "He is an honest, true, and brave soldier and gentleman. One who never faltered or hesitated in our long and perilous campaign. He deserves any favor that can be bestowed."[150]

None was by the War Department even though "Brigadier General Alpheus Williams led a division longer than any other in the Army of the Potomac."[151] The people of Detroit compensated for the lack of national recognition by erecting a magnificent equestrian statue of him and one of his horses—they were named Yorkshire, Major and Plug Ugly—on Belle Isle.

Just as overlooked, locked in an attic trunk and virtually untouched since the author's death, the papers of one of Michigan's generals were revealed in 1999. Orlando Willcox was a Detroit native. He graduated eighth of thirty-eight in the West Point class of 1847, ahead of A.P. Hill, Ambrose Burnside, John Gibbon, Charles Griffin and Henry Heth. A veteran of Mexican and other conflicts, he was an obvious choice to head up the three-months' regiment that answered the call for volunteers after Fort Sumter. Wounded and captured at First Bull Run, he was exchanged and returned to a hero's welcome in Detroit in August 1862 after thirteen months' imprisonment.

His remarks to the crowd are insightful, preceding issuance of the preliminary Emancipation Proclamation in September:

> *Here is a monster that lies curled up in our midst, and that threatens, with its scaly coils, to crush out freedom, and its name is slavery...There is no more need of talking about measures to put out slavery, or measures to protect the domestic institutions of the*

General Orlando B. Willcox.

South; for this war, with its thunder and its mighty revolutions, is of itself crushing out slavery, and you need not say anything more about it.[152]

In the thick of fighting, Willcox lost two horses to enemy fire at Antietam but was poised to strike a crippling blow against Lee's weak right when ordered (three times) to withdraw. He was acting corps commander at Fredericksburg and directed troops on the assault at Marye's Heights. After transfer to the western theater, he was stationed at Indianapolis in a support role but aided in the capture of John Hunt Morgan during the raid across the Ohio River in 1863. Restored to front-line command in March 1864, Willcox commanded a division during the Overland Campaign and at the Battle of the Crater. On August 19 at the Weldon Railroad outside of Petersburg, "Willcox and his division saved the day."[153] His sector was the target for Lee's final break-out attempt at Fort Stedman on March 25, 1865, and Willcox's troops successfully defended their lines. Within a week he led the breakthrough that impelled Lee's evacuation of Petersburg and Richmond, leading to the surrender at Appomattox on April 9.

The modern-day editor of his papers recaps: "Willcox had little, if any, political influence to exercise during the war, each of his promotions being earned by his seniority and merit alone."[154] From Bull Run as colonel of the First Michigan to the Civil War's end, from prison confinement to receiving the Medal of Honor, Willcox was the epitome of the nonpolitical general. His comparative lack of notoriety perfectly represents how history did not accord Civil War Michiganders their full due.

Other general officers with Michigan connections served without much fame but just as faithfully.[155] In the West Point class of 1846 graduated U.S. Grant, twenty-first out of thirty-nine. Five positions ahead of him was Christopher Columbus Augur, who had moved to Michigan when a boy. He served in the Mexican War and out West against the Plains Indians. The commencement of the Civil War found him commandant of cadets at West Point. In November 1861, he was promoted to brigadier general and commanded troops during the 1862 Peninsula Campaign. At the August 9, 1862 Battle of Cedar Mountain, he was severely wounded and subsequently received promotion to major general. He transferred to the western theater and served in the capture of Port Hudson, Mississippi, in July 1863. Brought back to head the Department of Washington, he escorted President Lincoln's body from the Petersen House to the White House after the assassination. It was an honor to a general who himself bore the scars of war.

Russell A. Alger, orphaned at the age of twelve, moved to Grand Rapids before the war to work in the lumber industry. Commissioned a second lieutenant in the Second Cavalry, he was involved in over sixty battles, wounded four times and led the first Union troops into Gettysburg on June 28, 1863. He was again wounded in the pursuit of Lee's army after the battle. At Trevilian Station in June 1864, his command "gallantly charged down the Gordonville Road, capturing 1,500 horses and 800 prisoners" according to Sheridan's report. At war's end, he received brevets as brigadier and major general. Resuming civilian pursuits, he moved to Detroit, where he became a leading citizen. He was elected governor of Michigan in 1884, was secretary of war in the McKinley cabinet from 1897 to 1899, was appointed and subsequently elected to the United States senate and died in Washington, D.C., in January 1907.

Israel C. Smith was born in Grand Rapids in March 1839. Enlisting as a private, he was promoted to lieutenant and captain, noted for bravery at the Battle of Fair Oaks in June 1862, wounded twice at Second Bull Run and once at Gettysburg and, on several occasions, exhibited great personal courage in the face of the enemy. He was transferred to the west in 1864 after recovering from his last wounding. Brevetted a brigadier general in March 1865, his postwar career was equally distinguished.

Henry Baxter was commissioned captain of Company C, Seventh Infantry, at age thirty-nine, on August 19, 1861. He was wounded in action at Antietam, led troops at Fredericksburg and received brevets as both brigadier and major general for gallant and meritorious conduct at the Wilderness in May 1864, Dabney's Mill in February 1865 and Five Forks in April 1865. He was honorably discharged on August 24, 1865, having served for four years and two days.[156]

And then there was Custer. Much has been written of his meteoric career—by one count, some sixteen hundred books. Among all of the general officers connected to Michigan, Custer garnered the greatest public exposure. He "was, in judgments handed down then and now, the ideal cavalry general," whose "leadership during the Civil War was nothing short of outstanding." His monument looms in downtown Monroe, signifying iconic status as the Michigan officer whose name would not have risen so high absent a post–Civil War end.[157]

Chapter 11

THE WAR POLITICIANS

The Civil War as a military conflict was largely staffed by civilians, not professionals. Critical to the North's success was the machine constructed to mold civilians into troops, train farmers and clerks into soldiers and arm and manage them. The Federal government relied on the states to mobilize and organize raw recruits into a land army that could overcome opposing forces—who were also American. The challenge should not be underestimated. In Michigan, a government apparatus that had ignored its militia before the war rose to the challenge. It was not unheard of even for some politicians to respond by themselves going off to fight.

Henry A. Wise is one better-known example to Civil War students. As antebellum governor of Virginia, he signed John Brown's death warrant. He served in the Virginia convention on secession and joined the Confederate army upon the withdrawal of Virginia from the Union. Commissioned a general in the Southern army, he was a brigade commander under Lee. Wise made his mark. Less known is a Northern ex-governor who similarly served his state in a military capacity and whose name was not far different.

Moses Wisner was born in New York in 1815. Moving to Michigan to establish a successful law practice, he purchased property in Pontiac in 1844 to construct an elegant home where he and his bride, Angeolina, lived quietly until events on the national stage drew him into political office. Wisner was a staunch Republican and Unionist.

A late nineteenth-century sketch summarized his career:

Governor Moses Wisner
(1859–1860).

In politics he was...a Whig of the Henry Clay stamp, but with a decided anti-slavery bias. His practice becoming extensive, he took little part in politics until after the election of Mr. Pierce to the Presidency in 1852, when he took an active part against slavery... On the passage of the Kansas-Nebraska Act of 1854, repealing the Missouri compromise and opening the Territories to slavery, he was among the foremost in Michigan to denounce the shameful scheme. He actively participated in organizing and consolidating the elements opposed to it in that State, and was a member of the popular gathering in Jackson, in July, 1854, which was the first formal Republican Convention held in the United States. At this meeting the name "Republican" was adopted as a designation of the new party consisting of Anti-slavery Whigs, Libertymen, Free Soil Democrats, and all others opposed to the extension of slavery and favorable to its expulsion from the Territories and the District of Columbia...Mr. W. was enthusiastic in the cause and brought to its support all his personal influence and talents. In his views he was bold and radical. He believed from the beginning that the political power of the slaveholders would have to be overthrown before quiet could be secured in this country. In the Presidential canvass of 1856 he supported the Fremont, or Republican ticket... In 1858, he was nominated for Governor of the State by the Republican convention that met at Detroit, and at the subsequent November election was chosen by a very large majority. Before the day of the election he had addressed the people of almost every county and his majority was greater even than that of his popular predecessor, Hon. K.S. Bingham.

His term having expired Jan. 1, 1861, he returned to his home in Pontiac, and to the practice of his profession. There were those in the State who counseled the sending of delegates to the peace conference at Washington, but Mr. W. was opposed to all such temporizing expedients. His counsel was to send no delegate, but to prepare to fight.

After Congress had met and passed the necessary legislation he resolved to take part in the war. In the spring and summer of 1862, he set to work to raise a regiment of infantry, chiefly in Oakland County, where he resided. His regiment, the 22d Michigan, was armed and equipped and ready to march in September, a regiment whose solid qualifications were afterwards proven on many a bloody field. Col. W's. commission bore the date of Sept 8, 1862...His regiment was sent to Kentucky and quartered at Camp Wallace...But life in camp, so different from the one he had been leading, and his incessant labors, coupled with that impatience which was so natural and so general among the volunteers in the early part of the war, soon made their influence felt upon his health. He was seized with typhoid fever and removed to a private house near Lexington...The malady baffled all medical treatment, and on the 5th day of Jan 1863, he breathed his last. His remains were removed to Michigan and interred in the cemetery in Pontiac, where they rest by the side of the brave Gen. Richardson, who received his mortal wound at the battle of Antietam. Col. W. was no adventurer, although he was doubtless ambitious of military renown and would have striven for it with characteristic energy.

He went to the war to defend and uphold the principles he had so much at heart. Few men were more familiar than he with the causes and the underlying principles that led to the contest...He was kind, generous and brave, and like thousands of others he sleeps the sleep of the martyr for his country.[158]

His valedictory address to the legislature in January 1861 contained this admonition: "This is no time for timid or vacillating councils, when the cry of treason and rebellion is ringing in our ears...Michigan cannot recognize the right of a State to secede from this Union. We believe that the founders of our Government designed it to be perpetual, and we cannot consent to have one star obliterated from our flag."[159]

Although Wisner's life[160] and career slid into obscurity, the war governor who occupied center stage for most of the conflict did not. On the east lawn of the capitol grounds in Lansing,[161] positioned to look down Michigan Avenue toward the rising sun, stands a statue of Austin Blair.[162] It is the only

Governor Austin Blair
(1861–1864).

monument of the seven on Capitol Square honoring an individual. The monument was commissioned by the legislature a year after Blair's death and three decades after the end of the conflict he helped win. One side contains speech selections; on the front is this inscription: "He gave the best years of his life to Michigan and his fame is inseparably linked with the glorious achievements of her citizen soldiers."

Why such an honor? A seminal work on the role of Northern governors suggests it is overblown: "In the long run Lincoln's victory over the governors was the triumph of a superior intellect…The other governors lacked the clear insight that Lincoln…displayed." Michigan's chief executive is last among those named with this summation: "Blair a fanatic lacking in political acumen."[163]

Fanatic? In 1848, he refused to support the candidate (Zachary Taylor) of his party (Whig) because neither was sufficiently antislavery, and he attended the more hospitable Free-Soil National Convention at Buffalo. In the state senate, he supported efforts to negate enforcement of the Fugitive Slave Act by voting for a personal liberty law. In 1854, he was a major force behind the meeting "under the Oaks" in his hometown of Jackson from which grew the Republican Party. He also served as a key draftsman on its platform. As a Republican delegate to the Chicago presidential convention in 1860, he supported William Seward of New York over Lincoln, believing the latter too soft on the slavery question.

Lacking political acumen? It was Blair who led the call for a unanimous nomination once Lincoln had enough votes to win:

> *Michigan, from first to last, has cast her vote for the great Statesman of New York. She has nothing to take back. She has not sent me forward to worship the rising sun, but she has put me forward to say that, at your behest here to-day, she lays down her first, best loved candidate to take up yours, with some beating of the heart, with some quivering in the veins (much applause)…We martial now behind him in the grand column which shall go out to battle for Lincoln.*[164]

As leader of his party in the state, Blair needed to turn out the vote for Lincoln in November. It was not close: 57 percent for Lincoln[165] to 42 percent for Douglas, with a paltry 1,220 votes for Breckinridge and Bell combined. The outcome put the state's 6 electoral votes in Lincoln's column and carried him over the 152 needed. Four years earlier, Fremont had the votes of much of southern lower Michigan except for Wayne County and Detroit. Blair carried that territory for Lincoln and more of the Lower Peninsula.

As governor, Blair offered military support to the president from the start. Before Lincoln uttered a word officially as commander in chief, Blair's January 1861 inaugural address pledged unqualified aid:

> *Secession is revolution, and revolution in the overt act is treason, and must be treated as such...I recommend you at an early day to make manifest to the gentlemen who represent this State in the two Houses of Congress, and to the country, that Michigan is loyal to the Union, the Constitution, and the laws, and will defend them to the uttermost; and to proffer to the President of the United States the whole military power of the State for that purpose...let us abide in the faith of our fathers - "Liberty and Union, one and inseparable, now and forever."*[166]

A year later, he led an effort calling upon Congress to increase pressure for prisoner exchanges—having in mind the return of the imprisoned colonel of the First Michigan Infantry. When midterm elections arrived in November 1862, the war was far from won. Democrats made comebacks in many states, but not in Michigan, where Blair's party remained strong as evidenced in this headline: "Michigan Elects the Republican State Ticket, 5 Republican Congressmen and One Democratic member, and a Republican Legislature."[167]

Some states saw a reversal of political power amid debate about issuance of the preliminary Emancipation Proclamation in September—Illinois, Lincoln's home state, included. Blair unequivocally celebrated the decision, having urged the administration to "confiscate contrabands" as early as January 1862. Since the antislavery efforts he had long sought were finally being employed, in 1864, he helped stem an insurgency within the party that threatened Lincoln's renomination. On February 4, he approved one resolution that recommended the president's reelection and one reaffirming Michigan's "unalterable attachment to the Government, the Constitution and the Union, and its undying hostility to the rebellion" with support of the national government to bring the war to a successful end. Blair also helped secure the ability of soldiers to vote in the coming national canvass.

The November 1864 election could have elevated Democrat George McClellan to the presidency, a result, in Lincoln's view, that would make winning the war impossible. The Michigan electorate faced a choice in the fall: reelect Lincoln and continue the current policy or opt for a different approach. Despite over three years of disheartening progress in the East and cognizant of the great strides made in the West, Michigan turned out for Lincoln again under Blair's leadership, casting 55.1 percent (91,133) of its vote to give him a second term (McClellan pulled 74,146). The state's electoral votes again went into the Republican column, and a Republican governor would take office again on January 1, 1865.[168]

With the war nearly won, Blair stepped down in 1864. He went on to serve three terms in Congress, during which he voted for the impeachment of Andrew Johnson. The speaker of the House of Representatives adjudged his service during this phase of his career:

> *He exhibited talent in debate, was distinguished for industry in the work of the House and for inflexible integrity in all his duties. He was not a party man in the ordinary sense of the word, but was inclined rather to independence in thought and action. This habit separated him from many friends who had wished to promote his political ambition, and estranged him for a time from the Republican party. But it never lost him confidence of his neighbors and friends, and did not impair the good reputation he had earned in his public career.*[169]

Blair had acted vigorously as the civilian commander in a mobilization of fully one-quarter of the state's male population.[170] When the War Department told him to cease recruiting activity since more troops were not needed, Blair ignored the injunction and kept on organizing regiments that, after all, were accepted into U.S. service when the need became obvious. He left office poorer than when entering it, for much of his personal funds were contributed to the war effort. His obituary in the *New York Times* summarized him: "famous as the loyal War governor of Michigan," the "Michigan Legislature, under his leadership, declared adherence to the government," after which he sent tens of thousands of Michiganders "to the field."[171]

His Republican successor, Henry H. Crapo of Flint, had supported the war effort as a legislator. Crapo managed the state through the final months of the

Governor Henry H. Crapo (1865–1868).

war and into Reconstruction until 1869. Upon taking the governor's office, he centered his remarks on the tens of thousands of Michiganders in uniform:

This is indeed a fearful sacrifice to be made even in the cause of liberty, justice, and humanity, and fearful is the penalty and terrible is the suffering which the authors and leaders of treason and rebellion deserve and must endure as a just consequence of this enormous crime. These brave men—the Michigan troops—are worthy of all praise.[172]

On June 14, 1865, he issued a "Welcome to Returning Troops" consistent with his inaugural:

> *Michigan Soldiers—Officers and Men:*
>
> *In the hour of National danger and peril, when the safety—when the very existence—of your country was imperiled, you left your firesides, your homes and your families, to defend the Government and the Union. But the danger is now averted, the struggle is ended, and victory—absolute and complete victory—has perched upon your banners. You have conquered a glorious peace, and are thereby permitted to return to your homes and to the pursuits of tranquil industry, to which I now welcome you! And not only for myself, but for the people of the State, do I tender you a most cordial greeting.*
>
> *In the name of the people of Michigan, I thank you for the honor you have done us by your valor, your soldierly bearing, your invincible courage, everywhere displayed, whether upon the field of battle, in the perilous assault, or in the deadly breach; for your patience under the fatigues and privations and sufferings incident to war, and for your discipline and ready obedience to the orders of your superiors. We are proud in believing that when the history of this rebellion shall have been written, where all have done well, none will stand higher on the roll of fame than the officers and soldiers sent to the field from the loyal and patriotic State of Michigan.*[173]

A year later, he performed a similar ceremonial role in accepting battle flags from Michigan's returned regiments.[174]

Zachariah Chandler was no mere ceremonial figure. The fire-eating Michigander's significance was, until recently, represented as one of the two Michigan monuments in Statuary Hall in the U.S. Capitol. He was mayor of Detroit before his election to the U.S. Senate in 1857, a strategist for and product of the Republican ascendancy in the state. He remained in that body until 1875, leaving to become secretary of the interior in the Grant administration. He also served as chairman of the Republican National Committee from 1868 to 1876.

Chandler cut a sharp political silhouette.[175] His election to the Senate "was due in no small degree to the belief of his constituents that in him

U.S. senator Zachariah Chandler.

they had found a man who would stand his ground, refuse concessions and demand recognition for the claims of the Northwest."[176] In response to the hanging of John Brown—a result he did not decry but turned to advantage—he fired a shot across the bow of the South: "I want it to go upon the records of the Senate in the most solemn manner and to be held up as a warning to traitors, come they from the North, South, East or West—dare to raise your impious hands against this Government, against our Constitution and our laws and you hang."[177]

When the so-called Peace Convention met to avert civil conflict in early 1861, Chandler led the Michigan congressional delegation in opposing concessions and compromises. He voted in opposition to the proposed Thirteenth Amendment that would have confirmed slaveholding rights.

Chandler "was unabashed in any mortal presence."[178] In a scene somewhat reminiscent of the 1856 incident where South Carolina's Preston Brooks attacked Charles Sumner of Massachusetts at his desk in the Capitol—but where he gave as good as he got—Chandler fought two South-sympathizing members of Congress from Indiana at the National Hotel in Washington. The donnybrook made him no less popular back home:

> *In his own State he found himself in thorough rapport with the people. Particularly in the country districts men, women and children came five, ten and even twenty miles to hear him, and it was no unusual thing, particularly in the new counties in the northwestern part of the State, for stores to close, sawmills to shut down, farm labor to be suspended and almost the whole population to turn out to the Republican meetings.*[179]

They were rewarded with stem-winding speeches that called for abolition of slavery and direct confrontation with the slaveholding power.

Chandler and Lincoln, though of the same party, differed on the slavery question. Lincoln wanted to contain it; Chandler wanted to eliminate it. Lincoln favored gradualism; Chandler favored immediacy. As early as the summer of 1861, Chandler was one of three leading senators pressing Lincoln to take steps toward a harsh war and emancipation.[180] Both favored a victorious conduct of the war, but Chandler was one of the major movers behind creation of a joint investigatory committee to hold accountable the administration, the military and those in supporting roles. On "every proposition to sustain the Administration with money and men he voted 'yea.'"[181] History calls him a "radical Republican," and when it came to prosecuting the war with utmost vigor, such a term was apt. He brooked no talk of easing up on the Rebels, as revealed in this example during debate on a resolution calling for retaliation for mistreatment of Union prisoners:

> *The Senator from Indiana objects to another statement that I made, which was that these Rebels are "hellish" or something to that effect. On reflection I think I have done an injustice, and no man is more ready to apologize for an injustice done than I am; but when I apologize for that remark it will not be to the rebels, but to the inhabitants of hell.*[182]

Notwithstanding his differences with Lincoln, Chandler worked in the 1864 presidential campaign to persuade John C. Fremont, the candidate of 1856, not to mount an intraparty fight for the nomination. Even though Lincoln had killed the Wade-Davis bill for Southern Reconstruction, which Chandler had supported, the senior senator from Michigan put the dispute aside.

> *Chandler induced Fremont to withdraw from the contest and secured the support of* [Benjamin] *Wade and* [Henry] *Davis for Mr. Lincoln. There is every reason to believe that Mr. Chandler's influence was potent in healing the breach in the Republican ranks.*[183]

Chandler's death in 1879 snuffed out a budding presidential candidacy. His legacy would be in a Senate career where he vigorously fought the "Slavocracy" and prodded the Lincoln administration to do the same.

The junior senator from Michigan during the war had, in common with his senior, an abiding hatred for slavery. Jacob M. Howard's style, however,

U.S. senator Jacob Howard.

was quite different. Soon after moving to Detroit from Massachusetts and securing a law license, he became Detroit city attorney and then a member of the state legislature. In 1854, he, too, was a key driver behind the formation of the Republican Party in Jackson and helped draw up its platform.[184] Howard was elected attorney general of Michigan and, in 1861, filled the unexpired term of the late Kingsley S. Bingham in the U.S. Senate. It was a substitution that would have far-reaching consequences.

Bingham was the first Republican governor of Michigan and a staunch supporter of its antislavery platform. It was Howard, though, who would do more in the Senate to eradicate slavery than his predecessor. Jacob Howard was "a scholarly man, a polished orator, an excellent constitutional lawyer and a highly respected citizen."[185] And he was a key supporter of the bill that became the Thirteenth Amendment to the Constitution, abolishing slavery: "I, for one, regard it as of the utmost importance not only to us but to our country and our posterity."[186]

Howard defended its simplicity and straightforwardness against all attempts that would complicate its meaning. In doing so, he relied on the formative document for Michigan's existence:

> *I wish as much as the Senator from Massachusetts [Sumner] in making this amendment to use significant language, language that can not be mistaken or misunderstood; but I prefer to dismiss all references to French constitutions or French codes, and go back to the good old Anglo-Saxon language employed by our fathers in the ordinance of 1787, an expression, which has been adjudicated upon repeatedly, which is perfectly understood both by the people and by judicial tribunals, a phrase, I may say further, which is peculiarly near and dear to the people of the Northwestern territory, from whose soil slavery was excluded by it. I think it is well understood, well comprehended by the people of the United States, and that no court of justice, no magistrate, no person, old or young, can misapprehend the meaning and effect of that clear, brief, and comprehensive clause.[187]*

That clause was ultimately adopted, containing simple words that constitutionally eliminated the underlying cause of the war: "Neither slavery nor involuntary servitude, except as a punishment for crime whereof the party shall have been duly convicted, shall exist within the United States, or any place subject to their jurisdiction." Both he and Chandler voted for it, and their state became the third to ratify it.

Howard was not done. A year after the war's military end, on June 13, 1866, Congress proposed the Fourteenth Amendment to the Constitution, guaranteeing citizenship to African Americans. The senator from Michigan was the floor manager of the measure in the upper chamber.[188]

Jacob Howard was a war hawk. When the question of elevating U.S. Grant to lieutenant general arose, he was completely supportive because of Grant's style and success: "Give us, sir, a live general…who will…give us victory."[189] He was a chief architect of the bill to provide for retaliation against Confederate mistreatment of Union prisoners. He may not have sounded like his colleague Chandler but in accomplishment was no junior.

Michigan's highest level of political leadership during the Civil War exhibited a number of common traits. They were pro-Union, prohard war, antislavery. They were looked at as radicals, and they did not shrink from the title. Soldiers had their support; slaves had their sympathy. These five had the courage of their convictions, and they led Michigan to victory.

Chapter 12

POWs: The Hard Life
and Andersonville

Orlando Willcox received his commission as colonel of the First Michigan Infantry, a three-months' regiment, on May 1, 1861. Before those three months were up, he was a prisoner of war and would be for many more. Though early in the conflict and far harsher conditions awaited captured soldiers later on, Willcox's experience is chilling. Commencing with the first significant battle of contending armies, North and South, Americans became POWs at the mercy of fellow Americans.

Treated well by his military captors and attentive medical staff near the Manassas battlefield, the recovering Willcox was soon transported by train along with other captives to Castle Pinckney in Charleston Harbor. The trip was an ordeal, "the worst by far I ever took."[190] Several times forced to stay in the cars for hours, with little food (mostly poor) and no water, the prisoners were "such a haggard set of wretches I never beheld."[191] After detraining at the Charleston station, they were marched not to a military facility but the town jail. Such treatment equated their status with common criminals—as the Confederacy soon classified them. They were held as "pirates and common felons" in retaliation for treatment of Rebel privateers up North.

While awaiting execution, Willcox found himself in solitary confinement on rations of bread and water. When the U.S. government relented on the privateers, his condition improved. He was moved inland to Columbia and confined to the city jail. Before long, prisoner exchanges commenced, and fellow officer William Withington—a "gallant Christian soldier and gentleman" who had rescued the wounded Willcox—was released.[192] As events progressed, Willcox and a contingent of forty Michigan soldiers were taken back to Richmond to await exchange. Initially held in a hospital, after several days they were confined to Libby Prison, where conditions were the worst he had endured.

Writing after the war, Willcox placed his time shuttling between prisons in perspective. The old tobacco warehouse was not Andersonville—site of thousands of deaths amid starvation—and he judged that Confederate POWs endured harsher treatment in Northern prisons. Still, ubiquitous filth and vermin made imprisonment a squalid experience. And another transfer, not northward to freedom but southward to Salisbury, North Carolina, inflicted

An unidentified Eighth Infantry soldier is pictured next to a sign that says, "Prisoner of War, Richmond."

emotional distress that exceeded any improvement in living conditions. Once more, his party was threatened with reprisal if prisoners at the North received a capital penalty. In August 1862, finally, Willcox was exchanged and transported into Union hands at Fortress Monroe.[193] He returned home to a hero's welcome.

Libby Prison was where Lieutenant James Wells, officer in the Eighth Michigan Cavalry, ended up after capture near Chattanooga in September 1863. He was marched to Dalton, Georgia, shipped in crowded freight cars to Atlanta, and then reshipped to Richmond. At Libby Prison, he waited vainly for exchange. After six months, he joined an effort to escape—a wildly successful one, for over one hundred soldiers fled to freedom. After a first attempt through a sewer failed, a cadre of prisoners worked for more than seven weeks on a tunnel from the east end of the prison basement, under a street, to the other side and a hidden exit. The prisoners went through the tunnel on the night of February 9, 1864, Wells among them. He and forty-two others successfully made the Federal lines. Going without food, crossing rivers and moving largely at night, he linked up with two other escapees and, out of resources, finally hailed approaching cavalry even though it meant taking their chances. The horse soldiers were Union, on patrol to seek out the escaped prisoners. Among those brought in was William B. McCreery of Flint, a colonel in the Twenty-first Michigan Infantry, wounded six times during the war.[194] Regained freedom for such men was very sweet.[195]

Wells hailed from Schoolcraft and had enlisted as a sergeant in December 1862. He was promoted to second lieutenant in March 1863; six months later, he was a prisoner. After his escape, he was promoted to captain in May 1864 and captured again during Stoneman's Raid in August 1864. This time, he was exchanged only a month later. His first encounter with prison life was trying: he was constantly hungry and suffered, along with many cellmates, from a feeling of unrest "which, if yielded to, often led to despondency and even insanity."[196]

Such experiences were not limited to a few Michiganders, and some had similar endings. Clement A. Lounsberry enlisted at Marshall in Company I, First Infantry, on April 22, 1861, for three months; he was eighteen. Like Willcox, he was wounded and taken prisoner at the Battle of First Bull Run. A year later, he was exchanged, whereupon he enlisted for a three-year term in Company I, Twentieth Infantry, as first sergeant. Promoted to second

Clement A. Lounsberry—thrice wounded, twice prisoner— enlisted at age eighteen on April 22, 1861. He rose to brevet major for gallant and meritorious services during the Overland Campaign.

lieutenant, he was again wounded and taken prisoner during the aftermath of the Battle of Chancellorsville in May 1863. Lounsberry returned to the regiment and was wounded in action yet again at the Battle of Spotsylvania in May 1864. He became a brigade aide de camp and assistant adjutant general, finally receiving promotion to colonel. Thrice wounded, twice a prisoner, Lounsberry received promotion and commendation for gallant and meritorious services during the Overland Campaign.

One of the most famous of POWs was Hazen Pingree. Born August 30, 1840, in Maine, he volunteered in a Massachusetts regiment and was captured at the South Anna River in 1864. Initially imprisoned in Virginia and North Carolina, he was transported to Andersonville prison near Americus, Georgia. When Sherman's march to the sea threatened the camp, Confederate authorities transferred him to Millen, Georgia. During a roll call for an exchange in November 1864, he assumed the identity of the other prisoner and escaped. Returning to the blue lines, he was present at Appomattox and had the pleasure of witnessing Lee's surrender up close and personal. After the war he moved to Detroit, began working in a shoe factory and started up a firm that grew into one of the best-known footwear manufacturers in the nation, Pingree & Smith. In 1889, he ran successfully for mayor of Detroit. In 1897, he was elected governor; forced to decide between retaining the mayoralty and governing the entire state, Pingree chose the Lansing post, where he served two terms.

Commissioned officers and enlisted men did not typically find themselves together. Lieutenant Colonel Frederick Swift of Detroit was captured at the Battle of the Wilderness. While being escorted to the rear and transported to a camp, he witnessed a Rebel general officer managing the battle. His captors confirmed: it was Robert E. Lee. En route to Georgia, he and a handful of others jumped off the moving train and hid out for several days, aided by a slave who provided food and guidance for their escape. Alas, they were recaptured and taken to a prison at Macon, where conditions were not as bad as Andersonville only because of the smaller number and rank of the inmates. Provisions were "very scant, poor corn-bread and worse bacon," yet the officers felt fortunate when learning of the privation at the other Georgia camp. To keep up their spirits, some men played whist, euchre, chess and checkers. Others died of despair and homesickness. Swift did not wait long for an exchange; taken to Charleston and locked up in the town jail for a time, he and companions later were placed under house arrest. Finally, the day of the ceremony arrived. The Union officers boarded a Confederate ferry, which steamed out toward Fort Sumter. Once safely transferred to a larger U.S. frigate, the prisoners rejoiced and were brought to tears when the blockading squadron outside the harbor lined up and fired salutes as their ship of freedom steamed past in review.[197]

Not all POW stories ended so joyfully. More than seven hundred Michigan soldiers and sailors never escaped, never were exchanged or never walked out of Andersonville alive.[198] From Fifth Cavalry soldier C.M. Abbott to John Zett of the Twenty-second Infantry, with artillerymen and engineers and sharpshooters included, the names of those who died there fill a dozen pages. The roster understates the effects of confinement, for others made it all the way back to Michigan only to succumb, literally in the arms of their loved ones.

Some four decades after the war, the governor—an escapee from Andersonville—and a delegation of legislators and dignitaries dedicated a

A bone ring carved by Thaddeus L. Waters, Second Cavalry, while imprisoned in Andersonville.

monument there, on Memorial Day, to those who endured and those whose final glimpse was of the walls of the prison stockade. The remains of two men were found while excavating the foundation for the memorial within those walls. Unlike several other states, the Michigan monument was situated not in the cemetery but on the ground where the prisoners lived and died. The governor recalled "the dense masses of the prisoners," remembered pitiless skies and suffering that day by day struck down the weakened "right and left." His remarks served as an epitaph for the sacrifice that all Michigan prisoners in all camps had made:

> *This is sacred ground, consecrated by the suffering of men who here gave "the last full measure of devotion."*
>
> *Theirs was not the glory of death on the firing line; the reaper touched them not amid the roar and the shock of battle. Penned in by the dead line, wasted by disease, far from home and loved ones, they were mercifully mustered out, leaving as a heritage to the nation the memory of a devotion as limitless as eternity itself.*[199]

Chapter 13

1864: Year of Ascendancy

The Union victory at Chattanooga propelled Ulysses S. Grant into the position of general in chief and command out East. He would face a new kind of adversary in Robert E. Lee, the Rebels' main hope for independence on the battlefield. The Confederacy was not limited to that route though, for November would bring an opportunity for voters in the North to determine whether Abraham Lincoln, or another candidate, would man the nation's helm in 1865. Peace was still a possibility and, with it, independence.

Something had changed, though, during these several years in the attitudes of individual Michigan soldiers. They were fighting for the Union, and they fought against the "slave power." What about freedom for African Americans? Perhaps, but in the spring of 1864, the Eighth Infantry demonstrated they were, indeed, fighting for a new birth of freedom. A Rebel slave owner appeared at their picket line outside of Annapolis, seeking to reclaim his runaway. The men of the Eighth "pounced" on the Southerner, who narrowly escaped with his life. He was no owner of property—he was the reason they were so far from home, seeing friends and neighbors wounded and killed. The Emancipation Proclamation, far from a divisive act splitting Northern brothers apart, had taken hold of their head and heart.[200]

An important factor in the *esprit* of Michigan units was a War Department policy that allowed special designations for those who had fought and would fight again. Charles B. Haydon of Kalamazoo, a practicing lawyer when the war began, had enlisted in the Second Michigan Infantry in April 1861.

James M. Greenfield, Seventh Infantry (Ontonagon County), enlisted at age twenty and reenlisted in December 1863. He was wounded in action at Meadow Run, May 31, 1864, and discharged for disability.

He fought at First and Second Bull Run, in the Peninsula campaign and at Fredericksburg. His unit was transferred to the West, where he suffered a grave wound at Jackson during the Vicksburg campaign. Fortunately, he recovered. Promoted to lieutenant colonel, Haydon became responsible for campaigning among his men to gain the designation of "veteran volunteers," a proud title signifying that they were not draftees and had reenlisted for the war's duration. It would only be awarded if a sufficient number of the men reenlisted, and they would be rewarded with a thirty day furlough. Haydon "campaigned strenuously for re-enlistment" and succeeded. Nearly two hundred re-signed.

In a diary he kept diligently during his service, Haydon bragged on his men. On the way home to Michigan to enjoy the furlough with them, he recorded this February 17 entry: "I have taken a very severe cold & am almost sick." It was followed on February 20 with an item about attending a theater play: "Everybody had a bad cold & coughed." There are no entries after February 21. On March 14, 1864, veteran volunteer officer Charles B. Haydon died of pneumonia in a Cincinnati military hospital. He had not lived to see his thirtieth birthday.[201]

After their respite, the Second was ordered back to the East. On May 6, it crossed the Rapidan River in Virginia and marched into "the Wilderness" with the rest of the Army of the Potomac. So named because of its dense tree cover, the thickets hid approaching Confederates who smashed into the Union right flank, commencing a running battle that would not cease for two weeks. Enduring thirty-eight casualties in the first two days, the regiment was ordered to march to the nearby courthouse town of Spotsylvania, where it went into action again on May 10, 11 and 12. At one point, the Confederates shot down every artilleryman in a New York battery and threatened to capture their four guns. The Second's commanding officer "immediately called for volunteers...who manned the guns, putting in a double charge of canister to that already in, and with these guns, loaded to the muzzle, opened a terrific and destructive fire" on the enemy.[202] The artillery was saved, as was the nearby Union line. It was the latest in a string of heroic exploits by the unit.

The famed Iron Brigade took part in the Battle of the Wilderness. Emile Mettetal did also. He had enlisted in the Twenty-fourth Michigan Infantry on August 12, 1862, at the tender age of nineteen. According to the company descriptive book, he was born in Redford, stood five feet, eight inches, had descended from French Canadians and was a farmer. A member of Company I, he had fought at Fredericksburg and other battles. After the Wilderness, he was declared missing. His name appeared on a different roll: the list of prisoners in the Andersonville camp near Americus, Georgia. He would be transferred to Camp Florence in South Carolina when Union troops approached. Early the next year, he would be paroled for reasons of illness and sent to Wilmington, North Carolina, for transport back north. He never made it. Although he may have died before leaving Florence[203] or Wilmington, Mettetal may have made it onto the steamer *General Lyon*, the transport for some six hundred prisoners back home. The ship was in a storm off Cape Hatteras and caught fire when the pitching waves tipped over kerosene barrels, causing the ship to sink. Only thirty-four made it to shore. Emile was neither on the passenger list nor among the survivors.

A great sacrifice was paid on May 12 at Spotsylvania by the Seventeenth Michigan. Its division was ordered to charge the enemy lines and take an exposed artillery battery. Advancing "under a tremendous shelling," it found itself confronting a larger Confederate force that was about to make its own charge:

The lines of the enemy extended in a circle around the left of our regiment, and closed on our rear, opening a heavy fire both in front and rear, at one time having the entire regiment prisoners. The men fought desperately hand to hand with the enemy, and during the

Roswell P. Carpenter, Twentieth Infantry (Ann Arbor), held ranks of first lieutenant, division ordnance officer and captain. He was killed in action on May 12, 1864, at Spotsylvania.

*struggle 43 men and 4 officers succeeded in making their escape...In
this charge the loss of the regiment was 23 killed, 73 wounded, and
93 taken prisoners, out of 225 engaged.*[204]

Never did men fight with more valor.

Spotsylvania was truly a bloody affair. One of the notable exploits on
the Union side was an attack by Colonel Emory Upton on the "Mule Shoe
Salient." Military experts have ever after lauded the brilliance of the assault.
Upton would later write the standard textbook on tactics for the U.S. Army.
Several aspects of the Spotsylvania attack were not noted as time went by. First,
it was not ultimately successful. Second, it was not originally Upton's idea. He
had received his early training as an artillerist under Henry Hunt—and thus
was a disciple of the teaching of concentration of firepower that Hunt had
demonstrated on several battlefields.[205]

Despite fearful losses in these May battles, Grant did not give up. He
continued to press Lee, seeking to maneuver him into a battle outside of
entrenchments where a decisive victory could be won. Lee countered every
move, until a surprising day when the Union forces moved swiftly and appeared
outside of Petersburg to the south of the Confederate capital, threatening to
cut off supply lines and forcing Richmond's surrender. The advance, however,
was botched, and Lee was able to thwart Grant's strategy. For a while, that is.
For the next few months, the Union lines around Petersburg and Richmond
would extend farther until they nearly reached and could cut off the rail lines
that supplied Lee's troops. On August 25, 1864, Michigan soldiers battled at
Reams Station, Virginia. Culminating a week of intense fighting outside of
Petersburg, eleven different Michigan units were involved in actions that left
many casualties, including Major Horatio Belcher of the Eighth Infantry. The
Flint officer had gone off to war three years earlier in August 1861; he was
killed on August 19.

In a bold move designed to break Lee's lines, Grant approved a plan for
a tunnel underneath the Confederate lines near Petersburg that would be
exploded and create a breach in their lines that Union troops could exploit.
The tunnel was dug, explosives were placed, a detonator was set off and tons
of earth and humanity were flung high in the air in an explosion that shocked
even its planners. The Union troops were ordered in, but they became
trapped inside the crater, struggling to climb up its unstable sides and facing

Confederates who surrounded the men in the hole and poured an intense fire into the hapless blue clads. Not all were overcome: "Among our troops was a company of Indians, belonging to the 1st Michigan S.S. [Sharpshooters]. They did splendid work, crawling to the very top of the bank, and rising up, they would take a quick and fatal aim, then drop quickly down again."

The Native Americans were not the only Michigan units involved, and they would all encounter a deadly situation together:

The sharpshooters, on the far left of the disorganized Union forces, were joined by the 2nd and 20th Michigan. They had gained a foothold on the Rebel works...Unit cohesion was impossible, and it is doubtful orders could have been heard, much less followed. Men clawed into the sides of the crater in a vain attempt to evade Confederate fire raining down on them. Under a pitiless sun, the corpses soon bloated and became breastworks for those who were still alive.

Through it all, the Indians kept their composure. Lieutenant William H. Randall of Company I, captured during the fight, remembered that "the Indians showed great coolness. They would fire at a Johnny and then drop down. Would then peek over the works and try to see the effect of their shot." Lieutenant Bowley claimed to have seen that "some of them were mortally wounded, and clustering together, covered their heads with their blouses, chanted a death song, and died—four of them in a group."[206]

Their sacrifice proved for naught; the Federals retreated, and Grant settled in for a siege.

In the West, the commander put in charge was William T. Sherman, and he was determined to take Atlanta. Second only to Richmond in military importance, the Georgia city was a railroad hub and armament supplier. Its fall would likely free Sherman's army to march northward toward Richmond and signify desperate times for the Confederacy. By a series of flanking movements, Sherman's forces maneuvered the Rebel army back into the outskirts of Atlanta. Several battles were fought en route, and at Peach Tree Creek, on July 12, Captain Frank Baldwin of Constantine, Company D, Nineteenth Michigan Infantry, won his first Medal of Honor by "leading a countercharge...under a galling fire ahead of his own men, and singly entered the enemy's line, capturing and bringing back 2 commissioned officers, fully armed, besides a guidon of a Georgia regiment."[207] Just nine days later, Battery F of the First Michigan Light Artillery was credited with being the first Union battery to throw shells into the Confederate stronghold.[208] Not long after, the city fell, and Union troops marched in. Back in Detroit, "amid great rejoicing an impromptu celebration was arranged. A national salute was fired, brilliant fireworks displayed, and speeches were made" by U.S. senator Jacob Howard and other community leaders.[209]

Sherman now developed a new plan: he would march to the sea, his target being Savannah, Georgia, making the South "howl." Leaving no military capabilities behind, Sherman ordered the depots, rolling stock and warehouses of Atlanta set on fire. The Michigan Engineers and Mechanics played a large part in obeying the order. The regiment also had a large role both in the march itself, by actively

John Henry Carpenter, Fourteenth Infantry (Washtenaw County), reenlisted on April 13, 1864. He was killed in action on August 7, 1864, near Atlanta.

opening roads and fighting when attacked, and in the opposition to the Rebel army that threatened Sherman's rear, by maintaining the railroads and aiding the capabilities of the Union contingent left behind to confront that army. A total of some three thousand soldiers would at various times be counted among the regiment. It would end the war with more men than it had at the start.

After the fall of Atlanta, Battery F of the First Light Artillery was sent back to Chattanooga, where it remained until being posted to Nashville. On October 26, 1864, the Twenty-eighth Michigan Infantry left for the front. Organized from communities in the southwestern Lower Peninsula, the regiment left its encampment at Kalamazoo for the Tennessee capital. In mid-December, it saw action at the Battle of Nashville, where the Rebel Army of Tennessee was crippled and put out of commission. Battery F, too, was in the fight.

The November election could have produced a result that, in Lincoln's judgment, would make winning the war impossible. The Michigan electorate—including its soldiers away at the front—cast their votes and decided on prosecuting the war rather than peace negotiations. The Michigan soldier vote was dramatically in Lincoln's favor. He won 9,102 to 2,959, a margin of 76 percent. Some were landslides: the Ninth Infantry went for Lincoln 413–95. The fabled and bloodied Twenty-fourth voted for him 177–49. Soldiers convalescing in hospital wards voted overwhelmingly for the Union ticket, 388–46. The war would continue.

It had been quite a year. At the start and for much of its duration, the prospects for the reelection of Lincoln looked grim. Michigan's political leadership helped clear the way for Lincoln's renomination, but a war-weary North faced a difficult decision. As late as September, Lincoln expected the worst. Then, Atlanta fell. If Lincoln's fate had depended on Michigan volunteers, though, he need not have worried. From war's commencement until the last day of 1863, Michigan had furnished 53,749 troops, enough for an entire army. Though an impressive number, the first ten months of 1864 proved more astounding. A total of 27,616 Michiganders were in uniform for the first time. The analysis: "The striking fact is exhibited by these figures that during ten months only of 1864 the State of Michigan had furnished more than half as many men for the service as were sent from the State during the whole of the first three years of the war, and of this large number of men actually furnished, only 1,600 were drafted."[210]

Far from surrendering to war-weariness, Michigan was stepping it up.

Chapter 14

CODA: APPOMATTOX, IRWINVILLE AND THE *SULTANA*

George Armstrong Custer reined up his mount, raised his eyeglasses and peered westward down the railroad tracks toward Appomattox Station. His scouts had reported that several trains waited at the depot, their box cars crammed with supplies for the approaching Army of Northern Virginia. Lee's troops were marching to this location as fast as possible in hopes of securing foodstuffs to enable their escape from the pursuing Federals. It was late in the day, April 8, 1865.

Escape? Pursuit? What had brought the armies to this rural Virginia countryside far from Petersburg and Richmond? After the Army of the Potomac had encircled its foe and both sides entrenched around the two cities in the fall of 1864, what developments had caused their evacuation that saw pursuer and prey racing down country lanes to Appomattox?

Over the winter and into mid-March, Lee's army had been continually stretched as Grant extended his left wing to cut the Rebel supply lines to the southwest of Petersburg. All of Grant's movements had been parried by Lee, but the extension of his trenches meant fewer Confederates could defend each section. The Rebel general knew something dramatic was required before flight became inevitable. He planned an offensive for March 25 designed to break through the Union lines, penetrate all the way to Grant's supply base at City Point on the James River and cause the Federals to lessen their pressure on his railroad lifeline. The point of assault would be Fort Stedman, part of the Union's entrenchments along the Appomattox River east of Petersburg.

The position of the Second Michigan Infantry lay between Fort Stedman and Battery 9. The men lived in holes in the ground covered by shelter tents, scarce protection from the fire of two enemy guns positioned across the river in front of the First Michigan Sharpshooters to the right. On the evening of March 24, Captain John C. Hardy of Detroit went out on picket with six posts of six men each. The wind was blowing stiffly from east to west, from the Union to the Confederate side, obscuring any noises in the Rebel works. Customarily, firing would continue all night every so often. At 1:00 a.m., all gunfire ceased. Hardy became suspicious of the quietude. He ordered a shot

John C. Hardy enlisted April 20, 1861, and was an eastern and western theater veteran. He earned brevet captain on March 25, 1865, for conspicuous gallantry in an attack on Fort Stedman.

fired from each picket post every three minutes to guard against a surprise. He also ordered men to crawl out of their pits and listen for any movement.

At 3:30 a.m., no longer content to wait on whether his premonition might be false, Hardy made his way back to alert the whole regiment that something was up. Some soldiers came running into the line without shoes or hats. Once gathered, it dawned on them that Fort Stedman had already been taken stealthily by a Rebel advance. Pickets were ordered in, and Hardy made his way to brigade headquarters through groups of gray soldiers who were rousting other Union soldiers from their sleep. Brigade commander Ralph Ely of Alma was informed of the situation and advised to proceed along the riverbank to where the First Sharpshooters lay, thus evading contact and enabling a surprise counterattack. Hardy made it back to the regiment and found it had taken refuge in Battery 9, prepared to reclaim Fort Stedman.

Once the brigade got into action, the Second Michigan found itself fired on from both directions. Other Union troops could not distinguish friend from foe in the predawn darkness. When daylight arrived soon after seven o'clock, and the Stars and Stripes could be plainly seen flying from the Battery, Union guns were trained solely on Fort Stedman and its Confederate occupants. A combination of artillery and small arms fire punished the Confederates; many began to flee back to the safety of their own trenches. A call went out for volunteers to "cut off the johnnies" and, with twenty-five men, Hardy dashed toward the fort. Finding a number of Rebels holed up, he called on them to surrender or be fired upon; with discretion the better part of valor, thirty-five Confederates surrendered. In total, over three hundred were captured by the regiment.[211] The fort was back in Union hands; Lee's final attempt at a strategic reversal had failed.

It was now apparent to Grant that the time was right to attempt his own breakthrough. On March 29, he began to apply pressure and, on April 3, reaped the reward when the Rebel lines in front of Petersburg were pierced. Union troops fanned out in both directions from the gap, taking prisoners and rolling up the Rebel defenses. Lee had to withdraw, and his only option was to pull the army out of the trenches and head west and then south in a forced march to link up with Johnston's force across the North Carolina border. The first blue-clad troops to enter Petersburg were the Second Michigan Infantry and the First Michigan Sharpshooters, which around four o'clock in the morning were into the city limits. At twenty-eight minutes after the hour, Michigan

The Second Infantry raises the U.S. flag over the Petersburg custom house on April 3, 1865.

soldiers raised the American flag above the courthouse for the first time in four years. Major Clement Lounsberry of Marengo accepted a flag of truce from city leaders, signifying their surrender of the town.[212] Petersburg was in Federal hands, and Richmond would fall within a short time.

As Lee desperately marched the army westward, hoping to elude his pursuers before they could prevent his link-up with Johnston, on his heels both north and south of the Appomattox River were Federal infantry and cavalry. At Sailor's Creek on April 6, a significant part of the Army of Northern Virginia was cut off and encircled.[213] Custer's Michigan brigade of cavalry participated under the command of Colonel Peter Stagg of Trenton, since the Boy General had moved up the ladder to division command. Lee's losses were devastating, nearly eight thousand men and eight generals. His army, now reduced to thirty thousand troops, continued westward in search of food and supplies on its altered and desperate escape route. Federal infantry kept nipping at his rear guard north of the river; south of it was Federal cavalry followed by more foot soldiers in blue.

On April 7, Lee hoped to secure food for his footsore and hungry troops at Farmville and then cross the river, burn the bridges and leave Grant high and dry. Before the supplies could be distributed and cooked, though, Union troops appeared on the same side of the river, east of the village, forcing Lee put his troops into battle until dark. The still-famished and fatigued army then began marching west again, toward Appomattox Courthouse and its nearby train depot, where food supplies would await them. Many had not eaten in

A ghostly image of George Allen, Twenty-sixth Infantry (Whitewater Township), who enlisted at age eighteen. He was killed in action in Farmville, Virginia, on April 7, 1865, two days before Lee's surrender.

a week. As an embedded *New York Times* correspondent put it while riding with the pursuers, Lee was "now making indecent haste toward Lynchburgh [*sic*], with the whole of Grant's army at his heels and left flank."[214] Who would reach the depot at Appomattox first?

On April 8, then, Custer knew he had won the race to the station. As he spied the locomotives sitting under steam at the depot, Custer knew that their capture could deprive Lee of his only hope at escape. The twenty-five-year-old general ordered his troopers into action, and between 8:00 p.m. and 9:00 p.m., an advance was made to capture the station.

The *Times* reporter would soon send a dispatch recounting the outcome:

Appomattox Station. Saturday, April, 8—10 o'clock p.m.

I have just witnessed another brilliant and successful dash by Gen. Custer, at the head of the Third Cavalry Division...The cavalry left camp near Prospect Station this morning...When the advance guard...had arrived within two miles of the station, it was ascertained that there were several supply trains on the track and a park of artillery in the vicinity. The advance...made a dash upon the station. Some 300 rebel soldiers made for the woods without firing a shot, leaving upon the main track and switches three large freight trains and one other train with locomotives attached and steam up. The engineer attempted to run the train off, but upon call moved the trains back to the depot again. Men were at once found... capable of running engines, who were detached to take the trains... to a place of safety. Three long trains filled with supplies of all kinds were thus run off before the enemy could recover from their first surprise, and a fourth was subsequently burned, with the depot.

The credit of stopping the trains is immediately due to Lieut. Norvall [Churchill], of Custer's Staff, who, being with the advance guard, saw the trains moving off, and taking half-a-dozen men, dashed up to the advanced locomotive, and brought the train to a standstill, by firing a couple of shots at the engineer. Norvall then run the trains back.[215]

Three hundred thousand provisions had been captured, enough to supply Lee's army for days. Without them, the Southerners were done in. To secure the railroad, Custer turned his attention on the Rebel artillery battalion protecting the trains and depot. He personally guided several assaults: "All the while, the general rode up and down the line, exposing himself to enemy fire, and cheering his soldiers on."[216] In a final charge, the Confederates were overcome. Custer's force captured thirty artillery pieces, a thousand prisoners and 150 to 200 wagons. Those cannons and wagons that did escape fled to the west, critically away from Lee. Custer's superior, Phil Sheridan, sent Grant a dispatch at 9:20 p.m., advising of the action: "Custer, who had the advance, made a dash at the station, capturing four trains of supplies with locomotives.

One of the trains was burned and the others were run back to Farmville for security."[217] The day's—and night's—action had paved the way for the encounter the following day, April 9, between Grant's cavalry and infantry, interposed from the west between the station and Lee's bedraggled soldiers at Appomattox Courthouse and the remainder of the Federal forces pinching from the east. Trapped, without provisions, nothing was left but surrender.

Lee's capitulation ended the main force in the field sustaining Confederate hopes for independence. It also meant the release of Federal prisoners accompanying Lee's army, who lacked food as much as their captors. A moving account was written by Major Farnham Lyon of Grand Rapids, quartermaster of the Seventh Michigan Cavalry, soon after the surrender:

> *I was ordered by General Sheridan to look up the cavalry train and bring it up, and was informed that it was in the rear of the Sixth Corps, which was directly opposite, in the rear of the enemy...When about two miles inside the Rebel camp I met the prisoners captured from us. When they saw my red necktie, which General Custer and staff always wore, one said, "There's one of Custer's staff officers," then such a shout as went up from two thousand Union throats is not heard every day.*[218]

That shout expressed the emotions of many in the North who would soon be engaging in celebrations of a similar nature.

A ceremony took place just a few days afterward, on April 14, far to the South. United States forces had recaptured Fort Sumter in Charleston Harbor in February. Lincoln ordered that on this Friday, the fourth anniversary of the surrender of the fort, the same flag that had been struck would be hoisted above the ramparts, signifying the restoration of United States authority. Robert Anderson, now a retired general, was present and spoke emotionally about the ultimate triumph that had taken so long and at such cost. Standing nearby, in attendance at Anderson's invitation, was another retired officer: Norman Hall. In 1932, a marker would be erected "by the United States...In memory of the Garrison Defending Fort Sumter during the bombardment April 12–14, 1861." Listed at the top was "Major Robert Anderson, First U.S. Artillery, commanding"; not far down is found this name: "2nd Lieut. Norman J. Hall."

SURRENDER OF GEN. LEE!

"The Year of Jubilee has come! Let all the People Rejoice!"

200 GUNS WILL BE FIRED

On the Campus Martius,

AT 3 O'CLOCK TO-DAY, APRIL 10,

To Celebrate the Victories of our Armies.

Every Man, Woman and Child is hereby ordered to be on hand prepared to Sing and Rejoice. The crowd are expected to join in singing Patriotic Songs.

ALL PLACES OF BUSINESS MUST BE CLOSED AT 2 O'CLOCK.

Hurrah for Grant and his noble Army.

By Order of the People.

A broadside orders "Every Man, Woman, and Child" to attend a celebration of victory at in Detroit upon Lee's surrender.

April 14 was fateful. That evening, at Ford's Theater in the nation's capital, John Wilkes Booth assassinated President Lincoln. As Booth escaped and fled southward, Michigan troops were brought into the dragnet. The Michigan Cavalry Brigade was ordered into the search and patrolled the countryside between Washington, D.C., and halfway to Fredericksburg.[219] Within a few days, Booth was trapped and killed. Other participants in the plot were apprehended, and two officers of the Seventeenth Infantry (the Stonewall Regiment), Major Richard A. Watts of Adrian and Captain Christian Rath of Jackson, "rendered important service during the imprisonment, trial, and execution" of the conspirators.[220] Rath is said to have put the noose on one of the prisoners, Mrs. Mary Surratt, the first female executed by the U.S. government.[221]

After Lee's surrender and the Lincoln assassination, forces under Johnston surrendered to Sherman in North Carolina. Confederate president Davis, however, did not give up. With the remnants of his government, he tried

Julian G. Dickinson, Fourth Cavalry (Jackson), earned brevet captain, U.S. Volunteers, on May 10, 1865, for meritorious services in the capture of Jefferson Davis.

to escape to the Florida coast in a ship bound for Texas. Near Irwinville, Georgia—not terribly far from Andersonville—the 4th Michigan Cavalry discovered Davis's camp and, after a brief fight, took the Confederate leader prisoner. Colonel Benjamin Pritchard of Allegan County commanded the troops; the University of Michigan–trained lawyer was rewarded with promotion:[222] "The 4th gained a national reputation and a world-wide notoriety by the capture of Davis. It was the accomplishment of an eminently special and important duty, for the nation, so distinctive and definite in its character, as to render a like service impossible, giving it a place in the history of the war without a parallel."[223]

The action effectively terminated any prospect for continued existence of the Confederate government and prevented Davis, an unyielding secessionist, from acting as president in exile—temporary or otherwise.

Sheet music cover for "Flight and Capture of Jeff. Davis" by Wolf Erine, Detroit. It was dedicated to "Old Michigan."

The end of the great national crisis had arrived, and the "last embers of the southern republic had been stamped out."[224] The cost had been frightful. More than 90,000 Michiganders had gone off to serve their country during the four years of the American Civil War, and over 14,500 never came home—more than 1 in every 7, a figure that averages to nearly 10 deaths for each day of the war. Some of those fatalities came with great cruelty, and none more terribly than on the night of April 27, 1865, aboard a Mississippi River vessel. The steamer *Sultana* had taken on many hundreds of passengers more than its capacity, bearing Union troops northward to their friends and loved ones. The war-weary soldiers did not fear: images of home and hearth beckoned. At 2:00 a.m., near Memphis, the overloaded boiler exploded, the boat caught fire and the vessel sank all too rapidly. Nearly 2,000 died—almost 300 of them from Michigan units on the verge of their safe passage from the front.[225]

The SS *Sultana* with soldiers—many from Michigan—crowded on board before the disaster on April 27, 1865.

Now that it was finished, no Northern state proportionally had suffered more deaths from military service in the war. Of the states with the greatest casualties as a proportion of total population, Michigan was among the top four with Illinois, Indiana and Iowa. The Twenty-fourth Michigan Infantry suffered a casualty rate of 80 percent on one hallowed battleground, "giving it the melancholy honor of the highest loss of any Federal regiment for the three days at Gettysburg."[226] The Twenty-second Michigan Infantry suffered losses of 85 percent at Chickamauga. Michigan units had been among those that sacrificed, in both the western and the eastern theaters, as much or more as any other unit from any other state.

Yes, the war was over. The Confederacy had been defeated; the Union had been preserved; slavery in America had been dealt a deathblow. Through it all, Michigan troops had served, fought, suffered, bled and died. At home, Michiganders had done their part. No one could quibble: Michigan had made "her great and bloody sacrifice for the Nation's life."[227]

Epilogue

FURLING THE FLAGS

They came from every corner of Michigan on the Fourth of July 1866, the ninetieth anniversary of the signature event that launched the American republic. There were no highways, no motor vehicles, only a few rail lines that linked populated areas, so they also came by horse, by buggy, by wagon, by walking. They came, men of different ethnicities, convinced that this muster was every bit as important as any they had attended. These soldiers of democracy came together; some had received a delayed birthright of freedom thanks in no small part to their own military service. They came because of their devotion to the nation, to the state that had fought its way into the Union and for the people who would not allow the permanence of the United States of America to be threatened.

They were "men set apart,"[228] these Michigan Civil War veterans. Some bore the scars of battle on their person: a missing hand, arm or leg; exhibiting a limp or shuffle or crutch. Others showed no visible evidence of suffering; still, in a tangible way, their wizened appearance conveyed a near-escape from death. Faded blue uniforms, careworn caps, tarnished brass buttons and well-trod boots proved who they were. Blue, yes, a sea of blue was massing this day, blue of those lake-bound shores, blue of the Michigan summer sky, blue of the field upon which the state coat of arms flew on flags they had followed into harm's way.

They shared a common bond forged in the storm of shot and shell of over eight hundred conflicts from Ohio to Florida and Pennsylvania to Louisiana.

Sergeant William R. Dodsley, Twenty-fourth Infantry (Detroit), Iron Brigade, enlisted at age twenty-two on August 5, 1862. He was mustered out on June 30, 1865.

That bond had been strengthened as they bivouacked together, marched together, shared privation and plenty together, endured temporary defeat and celebrated ultimate victory together. Now, with their mission to restore the Union accomplished, they gathered at Campus Martius, the drill ground and rallying point in Detroit for Michigan's militia since 1788, to perform one last act of service. In that public square, five years earlier, an enthusiastic crowd of citizens—men and women—had presented a set of colors to first responders of the First Michigan Infantry as they departed for war. Today, there was a mission yet to be completed: Michigan would be an early adopter of the Thirteenth, Fourteenth and Fifteenth Amendments to the U.S. Constitution, seeking to fulfill the new birth of freedom achieved by these soldiers and citizens. But on this July Fourth, a gathering of men and women made equally enthusiastic witnesses to the assembly of the blue-clad who would entrust symbols of the struggle into the state's care for all of posterity.

Attached to war-scarred staffs, regimental banners—altogether, there were 163 of them—were proudly borne into the square. Many were "mere shreds, tattered, torn and bullet-pierced," "illustrative of valor," "mementoes of patriotism."[229] There was that flag of the First Infantry, a unit in both battles of Bull Run. There was the scrap of the Twenty-fourth Infantry, illustrious component of the immortal Iron Brigade. There was the flag of the Eleventh Infantry that charged up Missionary Ridge into the teeth of Confederate fire. There was the guidon of the Michigan Cavalry Brigade, mounted troops who had evened the score with vaunted horse soldiers of the South. There was the flag of the Seventh Infantry that made an amphibious assault across the Rappahannock under fire of the Army of Northern Virginia at Fredericksburg. There was the banner of the First Engineers who had built the "Michigan Bridge" to open the key supply line to Chattanooga. There was the flag of the Seventeenth Infantry, the "Stonewall Regiment," who had charged up and over the wall near Antietam. There were banners representative of all forty-six regiments and several other independent companies, some proudly waving, others so fragmentary that were gingerly carried by hand.

For those flags that still could fly, their custodians felt the full honor of today's duty. All too many color bearers had carried these flags into the fight never to return; their graves, along with those of thousands who had followed them into battle or who had never emerged from behind prison walls, served as silent testimony to the gravity of this ceremony. As was now second nature, the Michigan men marched this day in rows and columns, orderly and straight, just as they had during the two days in May 1865 when passing in the victorious grand review of the Union armies in the nation's capital. They stood this day in those rows and those columns, orderly and straight, symbolic of the fallen comrades who now lay in rows and files, orderly and straight, in cemeteries at Gettysburg and Nashville and so many other hallowed places throughout America.

One of their own generals, overlooked for promotion despite his stalwart leadership, despite having served from First Bull Run to the final siege of Richmond, spoke for those veterans present and those unavoidably absent. Orlando Willcox reminded all of why these men had gone into combat: "not to establish or defend a throne, neither for spoils, oppression, nor any other unworthy object, but simply for the Union, and as soon as may be let the ancient foundations of the Constitution be restored with only the crumbling stone of slavery left out, and with liberty guaranteed to all." His voice rang out for the missing fourteen thousand, those who "return not to receive your thanks and the plaudits of their grateful countrymen. They walk the earth no more in the flesh, but their fame survives, and their glorified forms bend above us, now, and with hands unseen deck these colors with invisible garlands."

General Willcox concluded with timeless sentiments: "It only now remains for me, in the name of the Michigan soldiers, to surrender to the State these Flags, tattered but not stained, emblems of a war that is past. We shall ever retain our pride in their glorious associations, as well as our love for the old Peninsular State."

Governor Henry Crapo replied on behalf of the people of the two peninsulas: "I may venture to give you the assurance that you have the unbounded gratitude and love of your fellow-citizens; and that between you and them the glory of these defaced old Flags will ever be a subject of inspiration—a common bond of affection."

Battle flag of the Twenty-fourth Infantry.

Crapo spoke of the nobility of these "defaced" banners:

> *To you they represent a nationality which you have periled your lives to maintain; and are emblematic of a liberty which your strong arms and stout hearts have helped to win. To us they are our fathers' Flags— the ensigns of all the worthy dead—your comrades, our relatives and friends—who for their preservation have given their blood to enrich the battle-fields, and their agonies to hallow the prison-pens of a demoniac enemy. They are your Flags and ours. How rich the Treasure! They will not be forgotten and their history left unwritten.*

Concluding, the governor paid tribute to the raw heroism of farm boys and city clerks by making a solemn vow: "Let us, then, tenderly deposit them, as sacred relics, in the archives of our State, there to stand forever, her proudest possession—a revered incentive to liberty and patriotism, and a constant rebuke and terror to oppression and treason."

Within a few years, an imposing soldiers and sailors monument, designed by Ann Arbor native Randolph Rogers, would be erected in this square with monies collected from all over Michigan and aided significantly by efforts of its female leadership.[230] Four plaques containing bas-reliefs of Union leaders Lincoln, Grant, Sherman and Farragut—famed admiral of Hispanic descent— were featured. Four wingspread eagles stand guard below four women who symbolize victory, history, emancipation and Union. Crowning the fifty-six-foot-high memorial is an eleven-foot-tall female figure, armed with sword and shield, representing Michigan. Ever after at Campus Martius would stand this monument, "Erected by the People of Michigan in honor of the Martyrs who fell and the heroes who fought in defense of Union and Liberty."

Year after year, veterans of the war for the Union went to their final bivouac.[231] Some were buried in Detroit's Elmwood Cemetery, where the location of their graves fulfilled the promise of America. For here, next to one another, one finds veterans of all backgrounds, blacks next to whites next to Native Americans in a quiet pastoral setting that belies the titanic struggle they fought and won.

It was said so well on that Fourth of July: "while we have souls to remember, let their memories be cherished."[232] Indeed, their memory remains, yet today, our sacred trust.

ACKNOWLEDGEMENTS

No work of this kind is remotely conceivable without the aid of good people.

Deep thanks go to longtime assistant Jacqueline Tinney, who ably put together the manuscript; Sandra Sageser Clark, Michigan's historian, who lent helpful resources; State Archivist Mark Harvey, who supplied images from a treasure trove in the Archives of Michigan; and Michigan Historical Commission president Ed Surovell, who agreed to review the manuscript. I am thankful for Civil War students, reenactors, researchers, living historians and professional and volunteer instructors all across Michigan for their inspiring examples.

Nurturing an interest in history began very early in my family. Brother Tom recalls a 1963 trip to Gettysburg on an overcast day where three brothers sat enthralled in the back of our station wagon as a guide in the front seat regaled everyone with the lore of the battlefield. Brother Dave, the writer in the family, who helped strengthen this work, grew up to pen the seminal environmental history of the Great Lake State and launch a Michigan conservation historical marker trail. Appreciation of the passion for heritage instilled by my parents and grandparents is abiding.

Of Michael and Anna, no parent could be prouder, and none could have valued your encouragement on this project more.

Of Suzzanne, with whom a lifelong relationship deepened early during battlefield wanderings, you remain every day more than this husband could ever deserve.

Errors, omissions and sins herein are all mine.

Appendix

Roster of Michigan Units

1st Michigan Infantry (three months)
1st Michigan Infantry
2nd Michigan Infantry
3rd Michigan Infantry
4th Michigan Infantry
5th Michigan Infantry
6th Michigan Infantry
7th Michigan Infantry
8th Michigan Infantry
9th Michigan Infantry
10th Michigan Infantry
11th Michigan Infantry
12th Michigan Infantry
13th Michigan Infantry
14th Michigan Infantry
15th Michigan Infantry
16th Michigan Infantry
17th Michigan Infantry
18th Michigan Infantry
19th Michigan Infantry
20th Michigan Infantry
21st Michigan Infantry

22nd Michigan Infantry
23rd Michigan Infantry
24th Michigan Infantry
25th Michigan Infantry
26th Michigan Infantry
27th Michigan Infantry
28th Michigan Infantry
29th Michigan Infantry
30th Michigan Infantry
1st Michigan Colored Infantry
1st Michigan Sharpshooters
1st Michigan Light Artillery
1st Michigan Cavalry
2nd Michigan Cavalry
3rd Michigan Cavalry
4th Michigan Cavalry
5th Michigan Cavalry
6th Michigan Cavalry
7th Michigan Cavalry
8th Michigan Cavalry
9th Michigan Cavalry
10th Michigan Cavalry

11th Michigan Cavalry
1st Michigan Engineers and Mechanics
Source: *Michigan in the War*

Notes

1. Rockets' Red Glare

1. Bruce Catton, *The Coming Fury, Vol. I of the Centennial History of the Civil War* (Garden City, NY: Doubleday, 1961), 183, 186; Samuel W. Crawford, *The Genesis of the Civil War: The Story of Sumter, 1860–61* (New York: Webster & Co., 1887), 189, 375–76, 438, 457, 471; George W. Cullum, *Biographical Register of the Officers and Graduates of the U.S. Military Academy at West Point, N.Y., From Its Establishment March 16, 1802 to the Army Re-Organization of 1866–67,* vol. 2 (New York: D. Van Nostrand, 1868), 488; *Harpers' Encyclopaedia of United States History From 485 A.D. to 1906,* vol. 8 (New York: Harper & Bros, 1906), 473; Francis B. Heitman, *Historical Register and Dictionary of the United States Army From Its Organization, September 29, 1789, to March 2, 1903,* vol. 1 (Washington, DC: U.S. Government Printing Office, 1903), 490; *The War of the Rebellion: A Compilation of the Official Records of the Union and Confederate Armies* (*OR*) (Washington DC: Government Printing Office, 1880–1901), 23, 70, 71, 112, 137, 138, 150, 154, 161, 170, 179, 180, 201–02, 203, 211, 230; David M. Potter, *The Impending Crisis 1848–1861* (New York: Harper & Row, 1976), 570–83.

2. THE COMING FURY

2. The territory was established on January 11, 1805, with its capital in Detroit.

3. The Great Seal of Michigan features a coat of arms with a shield held by an elk and moose. Since Michigan touches an international boundary, a figure of a man standing on a shoreline shows his right hand that is raised in peace. His left hand holds a weapon, just in case. The phrase "*Si Quaeris Peninsulam Amoenam Circumspice*" is below these figures and is interpreted, "If you seek a pleasant peninsula, look about you." This may be a reference only to the Lower Peninsula, given an 1835 mindset, for the actual graphics were adopted at the original constitutional convention. Michigan political leader Lewis Cass created the design.

4. It also recognized the right to recover fugitive slaves: "Provided, always, That any person escaping into the same, from whom labor or service is lawfully claimed in any one of the original States, such fugitive may be lawfully reclaimed and conveyed to the person claiming his or her labor or service as aforesaid." On February 13, 1855, the legislature prohibited the use of county jails for detention of runaway slaves and directed county prosecutors to defend recovered slaves in Michigan courts.

5. Charles R. King, ed., *The Life and Correspondence of Rufus King, Volume I, 1755–1794* (New York: G.P. Putnam, 1894), 289–90. Draw your attention to the letter of Nathan Dane to Rufus King, July 16, 1787, on page 290.

6. Today's—mooted by the Thirteenth Amendment, but still a powerful statement of public purpose—says: "Neither slavery, nor involuntary servitude unless for the punishment of crime, shall ever be tolerated in this state."

7. On March 5, 1836, thirteen former slaves petitioned the legislature for authority to establish their own church in Detroit. It became known as Second Baptist Church, the first African American congregation in Michigan. The structure and congregation still remain.

8. Mull, *The Underground Railroad*, 49, 58, 70.

9. Michigan was a central player in this fight for American freedom, its proximity to the Canadian border playing a key role in making it so. The Michigan Freedom Trail Commission, constituted by Act No. 409 of 1998, continues to seek greater appreciation for the state's major role.

10. Mull, *The Underground Railroad*, 118.

11. *Personal Memoirs of U.S. Grant*, vol. 1 (New York: Charles L. Webster & Co., 1885), 193.

12. In the 1950s, the structure was moved to the Michigan State Fairgrounds to save it from downtown urban renewal.

13. The year 1848 was also significant because of another visitor. Abraham Lincoln had been elected to Congress, commencing in December 1847. Upon returning to Illinois from his first congressional session via the Buffalo-Chicago water route aboard the Detroit-built SS *Globe*, Lincoln's vessel became stuck on a sandbar near Fighting Island in the Detroit River. The episode inspired the young congressman to work on a model boat with inflatable bellows that would provide buoyancy in shallow water. After returning to Washington, Lincoln sought out an attorney and filed an application for a patent on his invention. U.S. Patent No. 6,469 for "Buoying Vessels over Shoals" was issued on May 22, 1849, influenced by a trip up the Detroit River. Lincoln is the only U.S. president to hold a patent.

14. Today what is left of the "Republican Oaks," then at the town outskirts, can be found near the northwest corner of Franklin and Second Streets in the city of Jackson. A state historical marker and other signage denote the location; an inscription reads "Here, under the oaks, July 6th, 1854, was born the Republican Party, destined in the throes of civil strife to abolish slavery, vindicate democracy, and perpetuate the Union."

15. Allan Carpenter, *Enchantment of America: Michigan* (Chicago: Children's Press, 1964), 36–38.

16. His one term as governor saw construction of the first Soo Locks, the failure of the legislature to approve his proposal to admit women to the University of Michigan and embezzlement of public funds by the state treasurer.

17. A Michigan historical marker commemorates the meeting place.

18. As recorded by the eighth decennial census. No enslaved persons were recorded, since slavery had been prohibited by the Northwest Ordinance of 1787 and the Michigan Constitution of 1835. New York had four times the population and Pennsylvania nearly that, Ohio three times, Illinois more than twice and Indiana nearly twice. Northern states admitted after Michigan before 1860 were Iowa (1846), Wisconsin (1848), California (1850), Minnesota (1858) and Oregon (1859).

19. The platform contained this statement:

That the maintenance of the principles promulgated in the Declaration of Independence and embodied in the Federal Constitution, "That all men are created equal; that they are endowed by their Creator with certain inalienable rights; that among these are life, liberty, and the pursuit of happiness; that to secure these rights, governments are instituted among men, deriving their just powers from the consent of the governed," is essential to the preservation of our Republican institutions; and that the Federal Constitution, the Rights of the States, and the Union of the States, must and shall be preserved.

It also contained this plank, reminiscent of how Michigan, part of the Northwest Territory, had been home to a ban on slavery from the foundation of the republic:

That the normal condition of all the territory of the United States is that of freedom; That as our Republican fathers, when they had abolished Slavery in all our national territory, ordained that "no person should be deprived of life, liberty, or property, without due process of law," it becomes our duty, by legislation, whenever such legislation is necessary, to maintain this provision of the Constitution against all attempts to violate it; and we deny the authority of Congress, of a territorial legislature, or of any individuals, to give legal existence to Slavery in any Territory of the United States.

Illinois, of course, was also covered by that Northwest Ordinance. The platform also rested on this pillar: "That we brand the recent re-opening of the African slave-trade, under the cover of our national flag, aided by perversions of judicial power, as a crime against humanity and a burning shame to our country and age; and we call upon Congress to take prompt and efficient measures for the total and final suppression of that execrable traffic."

20. Others who sought to get out the Michigan antislavery vote at campaign stops were Salmon P. Chase of Ohio and William H. Garrison of New York.

21. Doris Kearns Goodwin, *Team of Rivals: The Political Genius of Abraham Lincoln* (New York: Simon & Schuster, 2005), 268. In the book, Goodwin notes that a crowd of fifty thousand heard Seward speak in Detroit and that enthusiasm rose as Seward traveled west. She writes that "thousands waited past midnight for the

arrival of his train in Kalamazoo, and when he disembarked, crowds followed him along the streets to the place where he would sleep that night."

22. More than California's, Iowa's, Minnesota's, New Hampshire's, New Jersey's, Oregon's, Rhode Island's, Vermont's and Wisconsin's counts (and the same number as Connecticut's), not to mention certain states located in the South or along the border.

23. Twenty-four years to the day Michigan was ushered into the Union, Louisiana declared its withdrawal, becoming the sixth state to do so because of the 1860 election.

24. Kidd, *Riding with Custer*, 26. Here's how this Michigander wrote about him:

> *It was with something of veneration that I looked at this man...He did not seem to belong to the present so much as the past. Fifty years before I was born, he had been a living witness of the inauguration of George Washington as first President of the United States. He had watched the growth of the American Union from the time of adoption of the Constitution. He had been a contemporary of Jefferson, Madison, the Adamses, Burr and Hamilton...His work was done, and it seemed as if a portrait by one of the great masters had stepped down from the canvas to mingle with living persons.*

Cass remains one of Michigan's two representatives in Statuary Hall in the U.S. Capitol, having proven himself of greater presidential timber than the officeholder he last served.

25. Russell McClintock, *Lincoln and the Decision for War: The Northern Response to Secession* (Chapel Hill, NC: University of North Carolina Press, 2008), 40, 86.

26. Of all the thirty-seven states admitted later, Michigan remains the preeminent example of Congress requiring preconditions not found in the U.S. Constitution. Having had to negotiate their way into the Union beyond the customary admission procedure, it requires little imagination to envision how Michiganders became outraged when fellow Americans wanted to tear asunder the compact they had fought so hard to enter. Less than a quarter-century after its admission into the world's most elite governmental club, Michigan faced the prospect of eleven members deciding they would not continue their membership, would not continue supporting the continental defense, would "occupy" federal installations that citizens of every state, including Michigan,

had helped fund and garrison and would set up a rival polity based on the proposition that all men were not created equal. Michigan had been grounded on the opposite principle since 1787.

27. He would go on to raise the Twenty-second Michigan Infantry Regiment and serve as its colonel. Stricken with typhoid fever before ever seeing combat, he died at age forty-seven in Lexington, Kentucky.

28. Robertson, *The Flags of Michigan*, 27–28.

29. Silas Farmer, *The History of Detroit and Michigan* (Detroit, MI: Silas Farmer & Co., 1884), 305.

3. Answering Lincoln's Call

30. Robertson, *Michigan in the War*, preface.

31. *The First Call of the Civil War: A Paper Read by Gen. W.H. Withington Before Edward Pomeroy Post, G.A.R., at Jackson, Michigan, in 1897*, self-published, 5.

32. *The First Call*, 10–11. Seeing storm clouds on the Southern horizon, a number of militia officers lobbied for adoption of military measures, but their effort proved unsuccessful.

33. Robertson, *Michigan in the War*, 10.

34. *The First Call*, 10–11.

35. Robertson, *Michigan in the War*, 17.

36. Farmer, *The History of Detroit*, 966-67.

37. Robertson, *Michigan in the War*, 13.

38. Hoffman, *My Brave Mechanics*, 4, 6.

39. *The First Call*, 17.

40. Ibid., 19.

41. Ibid., 20.

42. Ibid.

43. This may be the occasion where Lincoln uttered "Thank God for Michigan!" though one history of Michigan's role in the war describes it as folklore. See Frank Woodford, *Father Abraham's Children: Michigan Episodes in the Civil War* (Detroit, MI: Wayne State University Press, 1961). It is the occasion when Lincoln remarked on the band leader's girth with "Professor, you must be the biggest blower in the service." *The First Call*, 21.

44. William Davis, *Battle at Bull Run: A History of the First Major Campaign of the Civil War* (Doubleday, 1977), 36.
45. Ibid.
46. *The First Call*, 22.
47. Ibid.
48. John A. Logan, then a congressman, fought at Bull Run as an unattached volunteer to a Michigan regiment, returned to Washington, resigned his congressional seat and entered the Union army as colonel of an Illinois regiment that he recruited. Logan rose to major general and became the first head of the Union veteran's organization, the Grand Army of the Republic.
49. Robertson, *Michigan in the War*, 20.

4. 1862: Swings of the Pendulum

50. Sources for this chapter are multiple, chief among them Robertson's *Michigan in the War* and the *OR*.
51. The Michigan monument at Shiloh, erected in 1918, contains three Latin phrases: *"E Pluribus Unum," "Tuebor"* and *"Siquaris Peninsulam Amoenam Circumspice."* (The beginning of the phrase is today worded *"Si quaeris."*) It also bears this inscription: "More enduring than this granite will be the gratitude of Michigan to her soldiers of Shiloh."
52. Besides the Second and Custer, the First, Third, Fourth and Fifth Infantries and a unit of the Sixteenth were engaged during the long campaign.
53. While these major battles attracted much attention, other stories of the war were being made. On August 5, Thomas Williams, son of the antebellum mayor of Detroit, was killed defending against an attack by Confederates at Baton Rouge. He was a graduate of the 1833 class of the U.S. Military Academy and had seen action in the Mexican War, where he received two brevets for gallantry.
54. Brodhead was, at various times, editor and part owner of the *Detroit Free Press*, state senator and postmaster at Detroit. His small stone office and library building constructed around 1855 remains on Grosse Ile.
55. The Seventeenth was mustered at the Detroit Barracks in August 1862 under the command of Withington and consisted of raw recruits from field, workshop and schoolroom. One company was composed almost entirely of students from Ypsilanti Normal School, now Eastern Michigan University. With less than a

month of military training, the Seventeenth left on August 27 for Washington. The regiment was one of several Michigan regiments that first saw action in the eastern theater, was transferred to the western and then returned to the eastern for its final campaigning. Ultimately, its total casualty rate was 26 percent.

56. Michigan regiments present at the battle included the First, Fourth, Seventh, Eighth, Sixteenth, Seventeenth, First Sharpshooters and First Cavalry.

57. Other units included the First Engineers, Battery D of the First Light Artillery, the Thirteenth and Twenty-first Infantry and the Second Cavalry.

58. He survived the war and toured the nation, putting on drumming performances and telling of his experiences.

59. Other Michigan regiments present were the Second, Seventeenth and Twentieth in the brigade commanded by Colonel Orlando Poe; the Third, Fifth, Eighth, Sixteenth and Twenty-fourth Infantries; and the First Sharpshooters.

5. Women of War

60. She is the first black woman to be honored with a bust at the U.S. Capitol. The sculpture is on permanent display in Emancipation Hall, the underground visitor center's main space. Professor Margaret Washington of Cornell University, in her book *Sojourner Truth's America* (Champaign: University of Illinois, 2009), describes the great Truth as having moved to Michigan to be closer to the prewar action and counted Battle Creek as her beloved home.

61. Farmer, *The History of Detroit*, 310.

62. Letter from Nan Ewing of Hillsdale to Husband Mack Ewing, November 12, 1864, Archives of Michigan, http://seekingmichigan.org/.

63. *Michigan Women in the Civil War*, Lansing: Michigan Civil War Centennial Observance Commission, 1963.

64. Mary Elizabeth Massey, *Women in the Civil War* (Lincoln: University of Nebraska Press, 1994), 80. The book cites an article in the *Detroit Advertiser & Tribune* on February 25, 1863.

65. Robertson, *Michigan in the War*, 47.

66. The text reads:

IN THE SENATE OF THE UNITED STATES
April 1, 1884

Read twice and referred to the Committee on Pensions.
AN ACT
Granting a pension to Mrs. Sarah E. E. Seelye, alias Franklin Thompson.
1 Be it enacted by the Senate and House of Representa-
2 tives of the United States of America in Congress assembled,
3 That the Secretary of the Interior is hereby authorized and
4 directed to place on the pension-roll the name of Sarah E. E.
5 Seelye, alias Frank Thompson, who was late a private in
6 Company F, Second Regiment of Michigan Infantry Volun-
7 teers, at the rate of twelve dollars per month.
Passed the House of Representatives March 28, 1884.

67. Laura Leedy Gansler, *The Mysterious Private Thompson: The Double Life of Sarah Emma Edmonds, Civil War Soldier* (Lincoln: University of Nebraska Press, 2005), 209.

68. For example, Blanton and Cook's book reports she was in the assault on Marye's Heights at Fredericksburg. DeAnne Blanton and Lauren Cook, *They Fought Like Demons: Women Soldiers in the American Civil War* (Baton Rouge: Louisiana State University Press, 2002), 14.

69. Thomas Lowry, *The Story the Soldiers Wouldn't Tell: Sex in the Civil War* (Mechanicsburg, PA: Stackpole Books, 1994), 122.

70. C.E. McKay, *Stories of Hospital and Camp, by Mrs. C.E. McKay* (Philadelphia, PA: Claxton, Remsen and Haffelfinger, 1876), 124–25.

71. Along with a number of officers and enlisted men who served in the Union army she celebrated, the lyricist is interred in Detroit's Elmwood Cemetery.

72. Reynolds, *The Civil War Memories*, ix-x.

73. Shirley Leckie, "The Civil War Partnership of Elizabeth and George A. Custer," in *Intimate Strategies of the Civil War: Military Commanders and Their Wives*, eds., Carol Bleser and Lesley J. Gordon (New York: Oxford University Press, 2001), 198.

74. Farmer, *The History of Detroit*, 311.

6. War on Water

75. Bradley Rodger, *Guardian of the Great Lakes: The U.S. Paddle Frigate Michigan* (Ann Arbor: University of Michigan Press, 1996), 4. Much of this discussion is based on this book.

76. After a long and stalwart record, its fate was ignoble. Sold to a foundation for preservation in July 1948, not enough funds were raised for its restoration, and it was sold for scrap the following year. After having survived for more than a century, all that remains are artifacts at a museum in Erie, Pennsylvania, and at the Michigan Historical Museum in Lansing.

77. Claire Hoy, *Canadians in the Civil War* (Toronto, ON: McArthur & Co., 2004), vi.

78. For both sides, this replicated the brother-against-brother phenomenon of its neighbor.

79. John M. Browne, *The Duel between the "Alabama" and the "Kearsarge," in Battles and Leaders of the Civil War*, vol. 4 (New York: Century Co., 1888), 622–23.

80. Charles Moore, *History of Michigan*, vol. 1 (Chicago: Lewis Publishing Co., 1915), 47–48.

81. Robertson, *Michigan in the War*, 990.

82. Gilbert, *Hillsdale Honor*, x-xi.

83. Robertson, *Michigan in the War*, 988-93.

7. Special Forces

84. See Raymond Herek, *These Men Have Seen Hard Service: The First Michigan Sharpshooters in the Civil War* (Detroit, MI: Great Lakes Books, 1998).

85. See Hoffman, *"My Brave Mechanics."*

86. J.H. Kidd, *Personal Recollections of a Cavalryman with Custer's Michigan Cavalry Brigade in the Civil War* (Ionia, MI: Sentinel Printing Co., 1908), 53.

87. Driving into Monroe from the east, one is met by an imposing sculpture of great beauty and power, reminiscent of the Stonewall Jackson monument on Henry Hill at Bull Run. This staggering work is every bit the equal to the one at Manassas and perhaps superior for being more realistic. It also bears the distinctive necktie worn by its subject.

88. An excellent work showing the complexity of U.S. cavalry operations and military riding is James A. Ottevaer's book, *American Military Horsemanship: The Military Seat of the United States Cavalry, 1792 through 1944* (Bloomington, IN: Authorhouse, 2005).

89. Duane Schultz, *Custer: Lessons in Leadership* (New York: Palgrave Macmillan, 2010), 33, 182.

90. After the war, Churchill's talent as a horseman and performer during Fourth of July events in Michigan eclipsed memory of this episode—until recently. A monument was erected on the field at Hunterstown in 2008.

91. See Eric Wittenberg and David Petruzzi, *Plenty of Blame to Go Around: Jeb Stuart's Controversial Ride to Gettysburg* (El Dorado Hills, CA: Savas Beatie, 2006), 173; Jeffry D. Wert, *Custer: The Controversial Life of George Armstrong Custer* (New York: Simon & Schuster, 1996), 89.

92. Richard Hamilton, *"Oh! Hast Thou Forgotten"—Michigan Cavalry in the Civil War: A Civil War Memoir of Sgt. George Thomas Patten, 1862–1863* (Self-published, 2008), 107–13. See Edward Longacre, *Custer and His Wolverines: The Michigan Cavalry Brigade 1861–1865* (Conshohocken, PA: Combined Publishing, 1997).

93. Kidd, *Riding with Custer*, 148.

94. Union cavalry commander Alfred Pleasonton is partly responsible for Custer's outfit during the war: "I used to let my staff dress as they pleased." William Styple, ed., *Generals in Bronze: Interviewing the Commanders of the Civil War* (Kearny, NJ: Belle Grove Pub. Co., 2005), 125.

95. Eric Wittenberg, *Protecting the Flank: The Battles for Brinkerhoff's Ridge and East Cavalry Field* (Celina, OH: Ironclad Publishing, 2002), 71–72.

96. Bleser and Gordon, *Intimate Strategies*, 188.

97. Authored by Captain Marshall Thatcher of Company B of the regiment, "aid [*sic*] to Gen. P.H. Sheridan," the memoir was originally published in Detroit in 1884.

98. Francis Miller, *The Photographic History of the Civil War in Ten Volumes: Volume Four, the Cavalry* (New York: Review of Reviews, 1911), 310.

99. In *Annals of the War*, the 1879 collection of *Philadelphia Weekly Times* articles, is the account written by H.V. Redfield of the "Death of General John H. Morgan."

100. *Michigan in the War*, 719–20.

101. Kidd, *Riding With Custer*, 306.

102. Wiley Sword, *Sharpshooter: Hiram Berdan, His Famous Sharpshooters and Their Sharps Rifles.* Lincoln, RI: Andrew Mowbray, Inc., 1988), 9, 11, 23.

103. H.C. Parsons, "Farnsworth's Charge," Voices of Battle: Gettysburg National Military Park Virtual Tour, http://www.nps.gov/archive/gett/getttour/sidebar/farnsworth.htm (accessed on October 13, 2010).

104. Styple, *Generals in Bronze*, 256–69.

8. TURNING THE TIDE

105. Gary Gallagher, ed., *The Fredericksburg Campaign* (Raleigh: University of North Carolina Press, 1995), 120. The text is quoted from the Dunbar Rowland collection of Davis papers.

106. Robertson, *Michigan in the War*, 441–42.

107. Mercifully, it was positioned at the right of the Union line for the next two days of the battle and endured relatively little action.

108. Robertson, *Michigan in the War*, 179.

109. Ibid., 242.

110. Pulford had also been wounded and captured at Malvern Hill; after his release from Libby Prison and exchange, he was wounded at Chancellorsville. After Gettysburg, he suffered wounds at the Wilderness and Boyndon Plank Road.

111. *Michigan in the War*, 365.

112. *OR*, series 1, vol. 27, part 1, 435–41.

113. Amos's brother Henry became a captain in the Twenty-sixth Michigan Infantry. He was killed in action at Hanover Junction near the North Anna on May 24, 1864.

114. *OR*, series 1, vol. 27, part 1, 435–41.

115. Ibid.

116. Ibid., 998.

117. Farnsworth's sacrifice was, for a time, not forgotten. The remains of a coastal defense battery—carrying his name—constructed in the time leading up to the Spanish-American War still exist at the site of Revolutionary War–era Fort Constitution at New Castle, New Hampshire. Its neglected condition symbolizes the state of his fame.

118. Bruce Catton, *This Hallowed Ground: The Story of the Union Side of the Civil War* (Garden City, NY: Doubleday & Company, Inc., 1956), 295.

119. Ibid., 299.

120. The colonel would be wounded in action near Marietta, Georgia, on the Fourth of July, 1864, losing a leg.

121. Catton, *This Hallowed Ground*, 298.

122. Ibid.

123. *OR*, series 1, vol. 31, part 1, 479-81.

124. Robertson, *Michigan in the War*, 163. Sources for this chapter are multiple, chief among them this volume and the *OR*.

9. THE FIGHTING 102ND

125. The literature on the event is uneven. For example, one recent work (Bak, *A Distant Thunder*) suggests it was related to the draft. An insightful analysis (Kundinger, "Racial Rhetoric") tying the violence to party politics, the preliminary emancipation proclamation and fear relates how the media contributed to the event. Richard A. Bak, *A Distant Thunder: Michigan in the Civil War* (Ann Arbor, MI: Huron River Press, 2004). Matthew Kundinger, "Racial Rhetoric: The Detroit Free Press and Its Part in the Detroit Race Riot of 1863," University of Michigan, http://www.umich.edu/~historyj/pages_folder/articles/Racial_Rhetoric.pdf (accessed on October 2, 2010).

126. See Kundinger, "Racial Rhetoric," 2.

127. Smith, "The First Michigan Colored Infantry," 6. Much of the remaining chapter derives from this work.

128. Ibid., 7.

129. Ibid., 38.

130. Ibid., 41.

131. *Senate Journal*, 37th Cong., 2nd sess., July 15, 1862, 843–45.

132. A state historical marker memorializes the location on Macomb, east of Chene, on the grounds of Duffield School near Elmwood Cemetery.

133. Born in Union City, Michigan. He was awarded the Medal of Honor for his role.

134. *OR*, series 1, vol. 44, 421, 422, 435.

135. Smith, "The First Michigan Colored Infantry," 130.

136. The preceding account is based on *OR*, series 1, vol. 47, 1,030–31.

137. Carleton Mabee and Susan Newhouse, *Sojourner Truth: Slave, Prophet, Legend* (New York: NYU Press, 1995), 227.

10. THE GENERALS

138. For purposes of this chapter, distinctions between an appointment in the regular army and the volunteer army, and brevets, are not emphasized.

139. Edwin Coddington, *The Gettysburg Campaign: A Study in Command* (New York: Charles Scribner's Sons, 1968), 525; *OR*, series 1, vol. 27, part 1, 993, 1,011–12, 1,018–19.

140. James Jenkins, "Elon J. Farnsworth: The Story of His Life," speech at the installation of officers of Farnsworth Post No. 170, GAR, January 15, 1904.

141. Much of this paragraph derives from Edward Longacre, *The Man Behind the Guns: A Military Biography of General Henry J. Hunt, Chief of Artillery, Army of the Potomac* (Cambridge, MA: Da Capo Press, 2003).

142. Henry Hunt was far below Henry Halleck.

143. Longacre, *The Man Behind the Guns*, 168.

144. Bruce Catton, *Glory Road: The Bloody Route from Fredericksburg to Gettysburg* (Garden City, NY: Doubleday and Co., 1952), 319.

145. Styple, *Generals in Bronze*, 146–57.

146. Bruce Catton, *Mr. Lincoln's Army* (Garden City, NY: Doubleday and Co., 1951), 191. In the book, there is a reference to how Hunt "insisted to the end of his days" that Pickett's Charge would have been truncated well before the High Water Mark had he "been allowed to do what he proposed—keep the Federal guns out of action" until the commencement of the charge itself. Then Catton's assessment: "He was probably entirely correct." Of course, such revised history could have undermined much of the lore surrounding the Third Day at Gettysburg. Imagine the monuments today on Cemetery Ridge as a collection of cannon and Hunt's statue standing alone.

147. He deserves better from historians. As one example, Gordon Rhea's in-depth Overland Campaign series attributes to him (and Warren) the by-the-left flanking strategy that Grant ended up using to entrap Lee in the Richmond-Petersburg lines.

148. Today it is a battlefield hospital museum, connected to the National Museum of Civil War Medicine.

149. Lieutenant Thomas L. Livermore, quoted in Sam Abell and Brian Pohanka, *The Civil War: An Aerial Portrait* (Charlottesville, VA: Thomasson-Grant, 1990), 57.

150. Milo Quaife, ed., *From the Cannon's Mouth: The Civil War Letters of General Alpheus S. Williams.* Lincoln: University of Nebraska Press, 1995), 393.

151. Bradley Gottfried, *Brigades of Gettysburg: The Union and Confederate Brigades at the Battle of Gettysburg* (Cambridge MA: Da Capo Press, 2002), 351.

152. Scott, *Forgotten Valor*, 3–4.

153. Ibid., 6.

154. Ibid., 653.

155. The names that follow are not a complete list.

156. Elmwood Cemetery in Detroit and other cemeteries around the state are burial sites of several Union generals, among them: Thomas Williams, killed in action at Baton Rouge in August 1862; Steven G. Champlin, died of wounds, January 1864; David Stuart, wounded at Shiloh; Philip St. George Cook, father-in-law of Jeb Stuart; and Thornton Brodhead (whose office on Grosse Ile remains a state historic site).

157. Schultz, *Custer: Lessons in Leadership*, 181, 182. This recent military leadership study also judges him as "glorious—fierce, determined, daring, leading from the front, making snap decisions, guided by some kind of 'lucky star.'" Foreword by General Wesley Clark, ix.

11. THE WAR POLITICIANS

158. "1892 Portrait & Biographical Album of Genesee, Lapeer & Tuscola Counties," http://www.usgennet.org/usa/mi/county/tuscola/book/book141-146.htm (accessed on October 7, 2010).

159. Lanman, *The Red Book*, 147.

160. Charles Martinez, "Governor Moses Wisner," *Chronicle* 31, no. 2 (2008), 24. Wisner's father and grandfather fought on the U.S. side in the War of 1812 and Revolutionary War, and his son also joined a Union regiment (the Fifth) at Fort Wayne in Detroit.

161. The Civil War–era capitol was a wood frame building located several blocks away from the current structure that was dedicated in 1879. Fire would end the existence of this second government building, as it had the first. The comparatively small and simple capitol was where war decision making occurred in far less grandeur than the current home of the Michigan legislature.

162. Edward Clark Potter was a sculptor who worked from around 1883 into the first two decades of the twentieth century. As with so much history, his story appears to have faded with the passing of the years. He studied under Daniel Chester French, the genius who designed the statue in the Lincoln Memorial. He also gained the admiration of Augustus Saint-Gaudens, made famous by Civil War commemorative commissions including the Shaw memorial on Boston Commons. New Yorkers know his work from the two lions guarding the steps to the Main Branch of the New York Library. He also assisted French with several pieces for the Columbian Exposition. In the main reading room of the Library of Congress are sixteen statues said to be by the greatest sculptors of their day; Robert Fulton is by Potter. Potter is also sculptor for Blair at the Capitol and Custer in Monroe.

163. William Hesseltine, *Lincoln and the War Governors* (New York: Alfred A Knopf, 1948), 391.

164. "Abraham Lincoln and Michigan." Abraham Lincoln's Classroom, http://www.abrahamlincolnsclassroom.org/Library/newsletter.asp?ID=49&CRLI=129 (accessed on October 8, 2010).

165. Coincidentally, the vote total approximates the number of Michigan troops in the war that followed.

166. Lanman, *The Red Book*, 148.

167. *Fremont (Ohio) Journal*, November 14, 1862.

168. The Michigan soldier vote went more dramatically in Lincoln's favor. He won 9,402 to 2,959, a margin of 76 percent. McClellan won a few units (First Infantry, 121–109), but others were landslides against him (Ninth Infantry, 95–413). The bloodied Twenty-fourth, unit of the Iron Brigade, went 177–49 for Lincoln. Soldiers convalescing in the hospital voted for the Union ticket, 388–46.

169. James G. Blaine, *Twenty Years of Congress: From Lincoln to Garfield*, vol. 2 (Norwich, CT: Henry Bill Pub. Co., 1886), 288.

170. Lanham, *The Red Book*, 146. The entry indicates that 110,000 was the eligible number in the 1860 census.

171. *New York Times*, August 7, 1894.

172. Lanman, *The Red Book*, 185.

173. Robertson, *Michigan in the War*, 69.

174. Crapo did not serve in the military like his predecessor Wisner, but a descendant did end up connected to a "general." Daughter Rebecca married William Clark Durant; their only son, William Crapo Durant, born in 1861, became the famous founder of General Motors.

175. See Mark K. George, *Zachariah Chandler: A Political Biography* (East Lansing: Michigan State University Press, 1969); Harris, *Public Life of Zachariah Chandler*.

176. Harris, *Public Life of Zachariah Chandler*, 44.

177. Ibid., 47.

178. Ibid., 78.

179. Ibid., 81.

180. Allen Guelzo, *Lincoln's Emancipation Proclamation: The End of Slavery in America* (New York: Simon & Schuster, 2004), 46.

181. Harris, *Public Life of Zachariah Chandler*, 62.

182. *Congressional Globe*, January 31, 1865, 519.

183. Harris, *Public Life of Zachariah Chandler*, 80–81.

184. Allan Bogue, *The Earnest Men: Republicans of the Civil War Senate* (Ithaca, NY: Cornell University Press, 1981), 39. "Honest Jake" was "reputably the man who chose the name 'Republican.'"

185. Ibid., 64.

186. *Congressional Globe*, April 6, 1864, 1,448.

187. Ibid., April 9, 1864, 1,489.

188. Eric Foner, *A Short History of Reconstruction, 1863–1877* (New York: Harper & Row, 1990), 116.

189. Carl Sandburg, *Abraham Lincoln: The War Years, Vol. 2* (New York: Harcourt, Brace & World, 1939), 540.

12. POWs: The Hard Life and Andersonville

190. Scott, *Forgotten Valor*, 309.

191. Ibid.

192. Ibid., 319.

193. Ibid., 329. Willcox's exemplary leadership during such trying times was lauded by his comrade Withington as critical to bolstering the morale of all around him.

194. Robertson, *Michigan in the War*, 883. He had lost the use of one arm due to wounds received. General George Thomas commented with regret on McCreery's resignation from the army for disability from wounds. McCreery would write an account of his escape for a MOLLUS publication. William B.

McCreery, *My Experience as a Prisoner of War, and Escape from Libby Prison* (Detroit, MI: Winn & Hammond, 1893).

195. Captain Daniel Fransberry, First Michigan Cavalry, and Lieutenant Charles Greble, Eighth Michigan Cavalry, also escaped.

196. James Wells, *With Touch of Elbow, or Death before Dishonor* (Philadelphia: John C. Winston Co., 1909), 141. This account is based on Wells's autobiographical work and Joseph Wheelan's *Libby Prison Breakout: The Daring Escape from the Notorious Civil War Prison* (New York: Public Affairs, 2010).

197. Frederic W. Swift, *My Experiences as a Prisoner of War. MOLLUS* (Detroit, MI: Wm. Ostler, 1888).

198. *Report of the Michigan Andersonville Monument Commission on Erection of the Monument at Andersonville, Ga* (Lansing, MI: Robert Smith Printing Co., 1905), 5.

199. Ibid., 15–18.

13. 1864: Year of Ascendancy

200. Guelzo, *Lincoln's Emancipation Proclamation*, 87–88.

201. Sears, *For Country*, 361. The chapter heading is "A Valley Forge Winter."

202. Robertson, *Michigan in the War*, 200.

203. Some 2,800 unmarked Union graves are there.

204. Robertson, *Michigan in the War*, 381.

205. Longacre, *The Man behind the Guns*, 67. ("Hunt would feel that, in addition to plagiarizing, Upton had botched his theft.")

206. Gordon Berg, "American Indian Sharpshooters at the Battle of the Crater," *Civil War Times* (June 2007).

207. "Medal of Honor Recipients: Civil War (A–L)." U.S. Army Center of Military History, http://www.history.army.mil/html/moh/civwaral.html (accessed on October 1, 2010). Baldwin would win a second during the postwar era, one of four students at Hillsdale College who would receive the medal. Thomas W. Custer would also be awarded the commendation on two occasions.

208. On January 9, 1862, Battery F was mustered into Federal service at Coldwater. It left the state for Kentucky in March 1862. After months of service in Kentucky, the battery marched across the Cumberland Mountains to Knoxville in January 1864. In May 1864, it joined Sherman's Atlanta campaign and fought at Resaca and Kennesaw Mountain.

209. Farmer, *The History of Detroit*, 308.

210. Robertson, *Michigan in the War*, 53.

14. Coda: Appomattaox, Irwinville and the *Sultana*

211. *War Papers*, vol. 2, 217–28.

212. A. Wilson Greene, *Civil War Petersburg: Confederate City in the Crucible of War* (Charlottesville: University of Virginia Press, 2006), 252.

213. Lieutenant Elliott Malloy Norton of Wayland, who served in the First, Sixth and Seventh Michigan Cavalry, was awarded the Medal of Honor for meritorious service at the Battle of Sailor's Creek. On April 6, 1865, Norton rushed ahead of his column and captured the flag of the Forty-fourth Tennessee Infantry.

214. *Grant's Army: Record of the Operations of Our Cavalry. Another Brilliant Affair by Gen. Custer Capture of Three Railway Trains, 25 Pieces Artillery, 200 Wagons, &c., by the Third Division. Details of the Surrender of Lee's Army. After the Surrender Order from General Custer.* N.p., April, 20, 1865.

215. Ibid.

216. Chris Calkin, *The Battles of Appomattox Station and Appomattox Court House* (Lynchburg, VA: H.E. Howard, 1987), 36–37.

217. *OR*, series 1, vol. 68, part 2, 653.

218. Calkin, *The Battles*, 167.

219. James Swanson, *Manhunt: The 12-Day Chase for Lincoln's Killer* (New York: William Morrow, 2006), 253. In the epilogue to this work, the role of Lafayette C. Baker—who moved to Michigan as a boy and was described as "a Michigan man (his father being an early pioneer of Clinton county)" in *Michigan in the War* on page 155—is explored. Furthermore, Baker's cousin went on the lecture circuit to exploit his role in the Booth chase as well as that of his horse Buckskin, who, after his death, continued to appear on stage thanks to the work of a taxidermy student at Michigan Agricultural College.

220. Robertson, *Michigan in the War*, 155–56.

221. William Christen, et al. *Stonewall Regiment: A History of the 17th Michigan Volunteer Infantry Regiment* (Detroit, MI: Seventeenth Michigan Volunteer Infantry, 1986), 50.

222. A Michigan soldier by the name of James Vernor ended up with souvenirs of the Davis pursuit and capture. He spent fifteen dollars for a dressing gown—perhaps the one Davis was said to have used as a disguise on the fly. Upon his return home, Vernor went into the beverage business and perfected a soft drink using ginger in oak casks that became a Detroit institution.

223. Robertson, *Michigan in the War*, 684.

224. Catton, *This Hallowed Ground*, 397.

225. Jerry O. Potter, *The Sultana Tragedy* (Gretna, LA: Pelican Publishing, 2000), 199–260.

226. Alan Nolan, *The Iron Brigade* (Berrien Springs, MI: Hardscrabble Press, 1983, 256.

227. Robertson, *Michigan in the War*, 7.

Epilogue: Furling the Flags

228. Bruce Catton, *Waiting for the Morning Train* (Garden City, NY: Doubleday, 1972), 189.

229. Robertson, *The Flags of Michigan*, 5–6. These pages quote a May 17, 1877 letter of Governor Charles M. Croswell.

230. According to the National Park Service, it is "the state's foremost Civil War monument." Many other locations in Michigan feature monuments, some humble (the GAR monument on the grounds of the state capitol in Lansing) and some involved. For example, at the center of Muskegon's Hackley Park stands a seventy-six-foot-tall Soldiers and Sailors Monument, designed by an Italian-born architect. The monument bears this inscription: "Not conquest, but peace—To the soldiers and sailors who fought and to all patriotic men and women who helped to preserve our nation in the war of the rebellion."

231. In 1877, Michigander Will Carleton authored and delivered a special poem to Civil War soldiers at Arlington National Cemetery. The lengthy composition won widespread acclaim, prompting one listener to boast, "I have no recollection of the day when I felt so proud of my country and especially of my native State, Michigan, as I do at this hour." The poem is entitled "Converse with the Slain" and contains fifty-five verses.

232. All quotations from the event are from Robertson, *The Flags of Michigan*, 87–89.

Partial Bibliography

Michigan-Related Civil War Works

Anderson, William. *They Died to Make Men Free*. Berrien Springs, MI: Hardscrabble Books, 1980.

Avery, James Henry. *Under Custer's Command: The Civil War Journal of James Henry Avery*. Compiled by Karla Jean Husby. Washington, D.C.: Potomac Books, 2006.

Bailey, George W. *The Civil War Diary of George W. Bailey*. Colleyville, TX: G.R. Post, 1990.

Bak, Richard. *A Distant Thunder: Michigan in the Civil War*. Ann Arbor, MI: Huron River Press, 2004.

Baxter, Albert. "Grand Rapids and Kent County in the War for the Union." Chap. 53 in *History of the City of Grand Rapids, Michigan*. New York: Munsell & Co., 1891. Reprint, 1974.

Beeson, Lewis, and Victor Lemmer. *The Effects of the Civil War on Mining in Michigan*. Lansing: Michigan Civil War Centennial Observance Commission, 1966.

Bennitt, John. *I Hope to Do My Country Service: The Civil War Letters of John Bennitt, M.D., Surgeon, 19th Michigan Infantry*. Edited by Robert Beasecker. Detroit, MI: Wayne State University Press, 2005.

Benson, Charles E. *The Civil War Diaries of Charles E. Benson: Corporal, Company I, Seventh Regiment Michigan Infantry*. Edited by Richard H. Benson. Decorah, IA: Anundsen Pub. Co., 1991.

Bertera, Martin. *The 4th Michigan Volunteer Infantry: The Battle at New Bridge, Virginia, May 24, 1862.* Wyandotte, MI: Tillieagnes Press, 2003.

Bertera, Martin, and Ken Oberholtzer. *The Fourth Michigan Volunteer Infantry at Gettysburg: The Battle for the Wheatfield.* Dayton, OH: Morningside House, Inc., 1997. (Reprinted by Bertera with Kim Crawford. East Lansing: Michigan State University Press, 2010.)

Bitter, Rand. *Minty and His Cavalry: A History of the Saber Brigade and its Commander.* N.p., 2006.

Blackburn, George, ed. *With the Wandering Regiment: The Diary of Captain Ralph Ely of the Eighth Michigan Infantry.* Mount Pleasant: Central Michigan University Press, 1965.

Brown, Ida C. *Michigan Men in the Civil War.* Ann Arbor: Michigan Historical Collections Bulletin, 1960.

Burt, Mary. *The Boy General: Story of the Life of Major-General George A. Custer. As Told by Elizabeth B. Custer.* New York: Scribner's, 1901.

Christen, William. *Stonewall Regiment: A History of the 17th Michigan Volunteer Infantry Regiment.* Detroit: 17th Michigan Volunteer Infantry Regiment, 1986.

Cole, Maurice. *Impact of the Civil War on the Presbyterian Church in Michigan.* Lansing: Michigan Civil War Centennial Observance Commission, 1965.

Committee on the Impact of the Civil War upon the Lives of Women in Michigan. *Michigan Women in the Civil War.* Lansing: Michigan Civil War Centennial Observance Commission, 1963.

Committee on Small Arms. *Small Arms Used by Michigan Troops in the Civil War.* Lansing: Michigan Civil War Centennial Observance Commission, 1966.

Conway, James, and David Jamroz. *Detroit's Historic Fort Wayne.* Mount Pleasant, SC: Arcadia Publishing, 2007.

Crawford, Kim. *The 16th Michigan Infantry.* Dayton OH: Morningside, 2002.

Crotty, Daniel. *Four Years Campaigning in the Army of the Potomac.* Grand Rapids, MI: Dygert Bros. & Co., 1874.

Curtis, Orson. *History of the Twenty-fourth Michigan of the Iron Brigade, Known as the Detroit and Wayne County Regiment.* Detroit, MI: Winn & Hammond, 1891.

Davidson, James. *Michigan and the Defense of Knoxville, Tennessee 1863.* Reprinted, East Tennessee Publications No. 35, 1963.

Day, Judson II. *The Baptists of Michigan and the Civil War.* Lansing: Michigan Civil War Centennial Observance Commission, 1965.

Dunbar, Willis. *Michigan Institutions of Higher Education in the Civil War.* Lansing: Michigan Civil War Centennial Observance Commission, 1964.

Ellis, Helen. *Michigan in the Civil War: A Guide to the Material in Detroit Newspapers, 1861–1866.* Lansing: Michigan Civil War Centennial Observance Commission, 1965.

———. *The National Tribune: A Guide to Selected Materials of Michigan Civil War Interest.* Birmingham, MI:, 1968–69.

Freitag, Alfred J. *Detroit in the Civil War.* Detroit, MI: Wayne State University Press, 1951.

Gansler, Laura. *The Mysterious Private Thompson: The Double Life of Sarah Emma Edmonds, Civil War Soldier.* Lincoln: University of Nebraska Press, 2005.

Gerry, H.E. *Camp Fire Entertainment and True History of Robert Henry Hendershot, the Drummer Boy of the Rappahannock.* Chicago, IL: Hack & Anderson, 1903.

Gilbert, Arlan. *Hillsdale Honor: The Civil War Experience.* Hillsdale, MI: Hillsdale College Press, 1994.

Gilbert, Henry C. *The Civil War Letters and Diaries of Henry C. Gilbert, Colonel of the 19th Michigan Regiment, 1862–1864.* Transcribed by Alcetta Gilbert Campbell. Corvallis, OR: A.G. Campbell, 1991.

Grave Sites Committee. *Graves Registration Committee Register.* Lansing: Michigan Civil War Centennial Observance Commission, 1966.

Hamilton, Richard. *"Oh! Hast Thou Forgotten": Michigan Cavalry in the Civil War: The Gettysburg Campaign. A Civil War Memoir of Sgt. George Thomas Patten, 1862–1863.* N.p., 2008.

Harris, Samuel. *The Michigan Brigade of Cavalry at the Battle of Gettysburg; and, Why I Was Not Hung.* Rochester, MI: Rochester Historical Commission, 1987.

Harris, Wilmer. *Public Life of Zachariah Chandler, 1851–1875.* Lansing: Michigan Historical Commission, 1917.

Hawthorne, Frank. *The Episcopal Church in Michigan during the Civil War.* Lansing: Michigan Civil War Centennial Observance Commission, 1966.

Hayes, Frederic. *Michigan Catholicism in the Era of the Civil War.* Lansing: Michigan Civil War Centennial Observance Commission, 1965.

Hayner, C. Irene, ed. *Materials on the Civil War Recommended for Use in Schools.* Lansing: Michigan Civil War Centennial Observance Commission, 1964.

Herdegen, Lance J. *Those Damned Black Hats! The Iron Brigade in the Gettysburg Campaign.* New York: Savas Beatie, 2010.

Herek, Raymond. *These Men Have Seen Hard Service: The First Michigan Sharpshooters in the Civil War.* Detroit, MI: Great Lakes Books, 1998.

Hoffman, Mark. *"My Brave Mechanics": The First Michigan Engineers and Their Civil War.* Detroit, MI: Wayne State University Press, 2007.

Isham, Asa. *An Historical Sketch of the Seventh Regiment Michigan Volunteer Cavalry.* New York: Town Topics Publishing, 1893. Reprint, Huntington, WV: Blue Acorn Press, 2000.

Johnson, Benjamin C. *A Soldier's Life; the Civil War Experiences of Ben C. Johnson. Originally entitled: Sketches of the Sixth Regiment, Michigan Infantry.* Edited by Alan S. Brown. Kalamazoo: School of Graduate Studies, Western Michigan University Press 1962.

Katz, Irving I. *The Jewish Soldier from Michigan in the Civil War.* Detroit, MI: Wayne State University Press, 1962.

Keeler, Alonzo M. *A "Guest" of the Confederacy: The Civil War Letters and Diaries of Alonzo M. Keeler, Captain, Company B, Twenty-Second Michigan Infantry, Including Letters and Diaries Written While a Prisoner of War.* Edited by Robert D. Allen and Cheryl J. Allen. Nashville, TN: Cold Tree Press, 2008.

Kidd, James. *Riding With Custer: Recollections of a Cavalrymen in the Civil War.* Lincoln: University of Nebraska Press, 1997.

Kloos, James. *Grave Sites of Union Generals in Michigan.* Cleveland, OH: Classic Printing Corp., n.d.

Lanman, Charles. *The Red Book of Michigan: A Civil, Military and Biographical History.* Detroit, MI: E.B. Smith and Co., 1871.

Lee, William O. *Personal and Historical Sketches and Facial History of and by Members of the Seventh Regiment Michigan Volunteer Cavalry.* Detroit, MI: Detroit Book Press, 1990.

Longacre, Edward. *Custer and His Wolverines: The Michigan Cavalry Brigade 1861-1865.* Conshohocken, PA: Combined Publishing, 1997.

———. *The Man Behind the Guns: A Biography of General Henry Jackson Hunt, Chief of Artillery, Army of the Potomac.* South Brunswick, NJ: A.S. Barnes, 1977.

Macmillan, Margaret. *The Methodist Episcopal Church in Michigan During the Civil War.* Lansing: Michigan Civil War Centennial Observance Commission, 1965.

Marks, Joseph, ed. *Effects of the Civil War on Farming in Michigan.* Lansing: Michigan Civil War Centennial Observance Commission, 1965.

Mason, Jack C. *Until Antietam: The Life and Letters of Major General Israel B. Richardson, U.S. Army*. Carbondale, IL: Southern Illinois University, 2009.

Mason, Philip, and Paul Pentecost. *From Bull Run to Appomattox: Michigan's role in the Civil War*. Detroit, MI: Wayne State University, 1961.

May, George. *Michigan and the Civil War Years: A War Time Chronicle*. Lansing: Michigan Civil War Centennial Observance Commission, 1964.

————. *Michigan Civil War Monuments*. Lansing: Michigan Civil War Centennial Observance Commission, 1965.

Mayo, Perry. *The Civil War Letters of Perry Mayo*. Edited by Robert W. Hodge. Michigan State University Museum Cultural Series 1, no. 3. East Lansing: Michigan State University, 1967.

McCarthy, Bernard, Chancey Miller and Joseph Schroeder. *Elmwood Cemetery: The Civil War Veterans*. Detroit, MI: Elmwood Cemetery, 1993.

McRae, Norman. *Negroes in Michigan during the Civil War*. Lansing: Michigan Civil War Centennial Observance Commission, 1966.

Metcalf, Kenneth, and Lewis Beeson, eds. *Effects of the Civil War on Manufacturing in Michigan*. Lansing: Michigan Civil War Centennial Observance Commission, 1966.

Michigan Adjutant General. *Record of Service of Michigan Volunteers in the Civil War, 1861–1865*. Kalamazoo, MI: Ihling Brothers & Everard, 1905.

Michigan and the Centennial of the Homestead Act, 1862–1962. Lansing: Michigan Civil War Centennial Observance Commission, 1962.

"Michigan and the Civil War: An Anthology." *Michigan History Magazine* (1999).

Michigan at Gettysburg, July 1st, 2nd and 3rd, 1863. June 12th, 1889. Proceedings Incident to the Dedication of the Michigan Monuments upon the Battlefield of Gettysburg, June 12th, 1889. Together with A Full Report of the Monument Commission, and a Detailed Statement of the Work Committed to and Performed by It, and the Proceedings at the Various Regimental Reunions. Detroit, MI: Winn & Hammond, 1889.

Michigan Labor and the Civil War. Lansing: Michigan Civil War Centennial Observance Commission, 1964.

Millbrook, Minnie. *A Study in Valor; Michigan Medal of Honor Winners in the Civil War*. Lansing: Michigan Civil War Centennial Observance Commission, 1966.

————, ed. *Twice Told Tales of Michigan and Her Soldiers in The Civil War*. Lansing: Michigan Civil War Centennial Observance Commission, 1966.

Miller, Chancey. *Elmwood Cemetery: The Civil War Generals*. Detroit, MI: Elmwood Cemetery, n.d.

Mull, Carol. *The Underground Railroad in Michigan*. Jefferson, NC: McFarland & Co., 2010.

Peckham, Howard. *Chronological List of Battles of the Civil War Showing the Particular Michigan Units Involved*. Lansing: Michigan Civil War Centennial Observance Commission, 1960.

Petz, Weldon, and Roger Rosentreter. "Seeking Lincoln in Michigan: A Remembrance Trail." *Michigan History Magazine* (2009).

Poremba, David L., ed. *If I Am Found Dead: Michigan Voices from the Civil War*. Ann Arbor, MI: Ann Arbor Media Group, 2006.

Quaife, Milo, ed. *From the Cannon's Mouth: The Civil War Letters of General Alpheus S. Williams*. Lincoln: University of Nebraska Press, 1995.

Reid-Green, Marcia. *Letters Home: Henry Matrau of the Iron Brigade*. Lincoln: University of Nebraska Press, 1993.

Report of the Michigan Andersonville Monument Commission on Erection of the Monument at Andersonville, Ga. Lansing, MI: Robert Smith Printing Co., 1905.

Reynolds, Arlene. *The Civil War Memories of Elizabeth Bacon Custer*. Austin: University of Texas Press, 1994.

Riggs, David. *East of Gettysburg: Custer vs Stuart*. Fort Collins: Old Army Press, 1970.

Robertson, John. *The Flags of Michigan*. Lansing, MI: W.S. George & Co., 1877.
————. *Michigan in the War*. Revised edition. Lansing, MI: W.S. George & Co., 1882.

Rodgers, Bradley. *Guardian of the Great Lakes: The U.S. Paddle Frigate Michigan*. Ann Arbor: University of Michigan Press, 1996.

Schultz, Duane. *Custer: Lessons in Leadership*. New York: Palgrave Macmillan, 2010.

Scott, Robert, ed. *Forgotten Valor: The Memoirs, Journals, & Civil War Letters of Orlando B. Willcox*. Kent, OH: Kent State University Press, 1999.

Sears, Stephen, ed. *For Country, Cause & Leader: The Civil War Journal of Charles B. Haydon*. New York: Ticknor & Fields, 1993.

Sexton, Jesse Ethelyn. *Congregationalism, Slavery and the Civil War*. Lansing: Michigan Civil War Centennial Observance Commission, 1966.

Shultz, David. *"Double Canister At Ten Yards": The Federal Artillery and the Repulse of Pickett's Charge.* Redondo Beach, CA: Rank and File Publications, 1995.

Sligh, Charles R. *History of the Services of the First Regiment Michigan Engineers and Mechanics, during the Civil War.* Grand Rapids, MI: White Print. Co., 1921.

Smith, Donald. *The Twenty-Fourth Michigan.* Harrisburg, PA: Stackpole Co., 1962.

Smith, Michael O. "The First Michigan Colored Infantry: A Black Regiment in the Civil War." Master's thesis, Wayne State University, 1987.

Starr, Thomas. *Lincoln's Kalamazoo Address Against Extending Slavery. Also His Life by Joseph J. Lewis.* Detroit: Fine Book Circle, 1941.

Teal, Mary, and Lawrence Brown. *The Effect of the Civil War on Music in Michigan.* Lansing: Michigan Civil War Centennial Observance Commission, 1965.

"Thank God for Michigan: Civil War Collector's Issue." *Michigan History Magazine* (1998).

Thatcher, Marshall. *A Hundred Battles in the West. St. Louis to Atlanta, 1861–65; The Second Michigan Cavalry.* Detroit, MI: 1884.

Thornton, Leland W. *When Gallantry Was Commonplace: The History of the Michigan Eleventh Volunteer Infantry, 1861–1864.* American University Studies Series 9, 0740-0462, vol. 90. New York: P. Lang, 1991.

Townshend, David G. *The Seventh Michigan Volunteer Infantry: The Gallant Men and Flag in the Civil War, 1861 to 1865.* Fort Lauderdale, FL: Southeast Publications, 1993.

Urwin, Gregory. *Custer Victorious: The Civil War Battles of General George Armstrong Custer.* Lincoln: University of Nebraska Press, 1983.

The U.S. Grant House, Detroit, Michigan. Detroit, MI: Detroit Historical Society and Michigan Mutual Ins. Co., 1978.

Vale, Joseph. *Minty and the Cavalry: A History of Cavalry Campaigns in the Western Armies.* Harrisburg, PA: Edwin K. Meyers, 1886.

War Papers Read Before the Commandery of the State of Michigan Military Order of the Loyal Legion of the United States, Vol. 1. Detroit, MI: Winn & Hammond, 1893.

War Papers Read Before the Commandery of the State of Michigan Military Order of the Loyal Legion of the United States, Vol. 2. Detroit, MI: Winn & Hammond, 1898.

Weber, Daniel, ed. *From Michigan to Murfreesboro: The Diary of Ira Gillaspie of the Eleventh Michigan Infantry.* Mount Pleasant: Central Michigan University Press, 1965.

Welcher, Frank J., and Larry Ligget. *Coburn's Brigade: 85th Indiana, 33rd Indiana, 19th Michigan, and 22nd Wisconsin in the Western Civil War.* Carmel: Guild Press of Indiana, 1999.

Wichers, Wynand. *The Dutch Churches of Michigan in the Civil War.* Lansing: Michigan Civil War Centennial Observance Commission, 1965.

Williams, Frederick. *Michigan Soldiers in the Civil War.* Lansing: Michigan Historical Commission, 1960. Reprint, 2002.

Wilterdink, John A. *My Country and Cross: The Civil War Letters of John Anthony Wilterdink, Company I, 25th Michigan Infantry.* Edited by Albert McGeehan. Dallas, TX: Taylor Pub. Co., 1992.

Wittenberg, Eric, ed. *At Custer's Side: The Civil War Writings of James Harvey Kidd.* Kent, OH: Kent State University Press, 2001.

———. *Glory Enough For All: Sheridan's Second Raid and the Battle of Trevilian Station.* Washington, D.C.: Brassey's, Inc., 2001.

———. *Protecting the Flank: The Battles for Brinkerhoff's Ridge and East Cavalry Field.* Celina, OH: Ironclad Publishing, 2002.

Woodford, Frank. *Father Abraham's Children: Michigan Episodes in the Civil War.* Detroit, MI: Wayne State University Press, 1961.

Yzenbaard, John. *Civil War Tri-State Soldiers' and Sailors' Encampments: 1889–1918.* Lansing: Michigan Civil War Centennial Observance Commission, 1966.

INDEX

ABOUT THE AUTHOR

Jack Dempsey, former assistant attorney general for the State of Michigan, is firmly embedded in the Michigan Civil War community. He runs a popular Michigan in the Civil War blog and is the vice-president of the Michigan Historical Commission, as well as a board member of the Michigan History Foundation and the Historical Society of Michigan. He is also a color bearer with the Civil War Preservation Trust.

His website is http://www.micwc.typepad.com.

Visit us at
www.historypress.net